THE KNOT
OF ARTIFICE

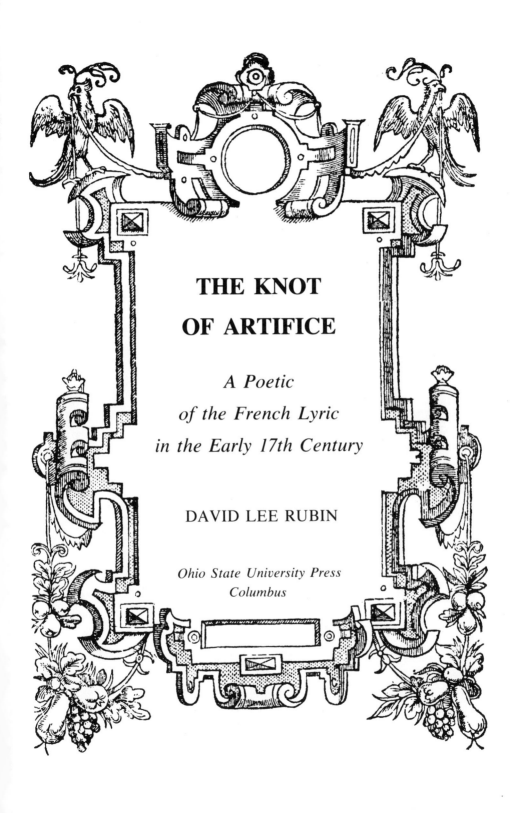

THE KNOT
OF ARTIFICE

A Poetic
of the French Lyric
in the Early 17th Century

DAVID LEE RUBIN

Ohio State University Press
Columbus

184112

Library of Congress Cataloging in Publication Data

Rubin, David Lee.
The knot of artifice.

Bibliography: p.
Includes index.
1. French poetry—17th century—History and
criticism. I. Title.
PQ421.R8   841′.0409   80-26260
ISBN 0-8142-0322-1

IN MEMORIAM

Bernard Weinberg

'skillful guide in poetic ground'

TABLE OF CONTENTS

Acknowledgments

For inviting me to present brief papers based on the early research for this essay, I wish to thank section officers of the Modern Language Association of America, the North American Society for Seventeenth-Century French Literature, the American Association of Teachers of French, and the Northeast MLA.

Preliminary versions of several passages have appeared in *Yale French Studies, Australian Journal of French Studies, Papers on French Seventeenth-Century Literature,* and the *Cahiers Maynard.* I am obligated to the editors, who have permitted me to reprint these materials, usually with drastic changes of evidence or argumentation.

For three fellowships that enabled me to devote full attention to the project, I am in the debt of the Committee on Summer Research Grants at the University of Virginia and the administrators of the University's Center for Advanced Studies.

No words can repay what I owe to Allan H. Pasco, Hugh M. Davidson, Robert T. Corum, Jr., Terence C. Cave, and Charles G. S. Williams, who read and judiciously commented on the entire manuscript; to Wolfgang Leiner, C. K. Abraham, Marcel Gutwirth, Francis Lawrence, Odette de Mourgues, H. Gaston Hall, Doranne Fenoaltea, Jacqueline Van Baelen, Claire Gaudiani, Robert Cook, Stephen Baehr, Carrol Coates, and T. J.

Reiss, who read or heard various analyses and responded with encouragement, constructive advice, or valuable information; to Roger Shattuck, A. James Arnold, Robert Nicolich, and Michael Issacharoff for enabling me to see the powers and limitations of my method, especially when compared with less differential approaches; to my students at the University of Virginia, especially Nancy Hafer, Catherine Ingold, Ann Elkin Rose-McBride, Janet Railton, and, again, Robert T. Corum, Jr., who tested and invariably refined my thought in discussions and papers, or their own diploma pieces; to the acute and enthusiastic participants in five MLA seminars that I organized to encourage formal analysis of the early seventeenth-century French lyric; to my past and present departmental chairmen, Lester G. Crocker and Robert T. Denommé, for their unflagging confidence; and to Weldon Kefauver, director of Ohio State University Press, as well as my editor, Carol S. Sykes, who treated the manuscript (and its author) with consummate professionalism and generosity.

For listening bravely eight years as I ruminated aloud and without end about this work in progress, I am grateful to my wife, Carolyn Dettman Rubin.

I, of course, must answer for all errors of fact and inadequacies of thought or expression that remain in the pages to follow.

THE KNOT
OF ARTIFICE

Fain would I dwell on form.

Romeo and Juliet 2. 1. 84.

Introduction
Motivations and Models

Despite a generation of conscientious study, lyric form in the age of Malherbe remains puzzling, mystifying, even baffling. We know little more about it today than did Lanson, when—in a teleological mood—he declared some poets of the period to be precursors of classicism but others, "attardés et égarés."[1] There are at least two explanations for this paradoxical state of affairs: the overwhelming preference of critics for integrative approaches to poetry, as well as the narrowness and atomism of many differential methods.[2]

REFERENCE AND THE CHARACTERISTIC

The procedure of integrative criticism is threefold: first, it refers or analogizes literature to extrapoetic causes or qualities, to other arts, or to the behavioral sciences; from this synthesis it derives appropriate sets of categories, most frequently, antithetical; finally, it relates characteristic features of works and genres to the preestablished paradigm. The text is thus rediscovered in a cultural context: that of its creation or its reception. In their systematic application to the telling detail, however, the various modes of integrative criticism deemphasize the poem as a potentially complete and coherent object interesting in and for itself. This choice is defensible, of course, on grounds of intellectual economy, a virtue consonant with the methods' enviable rigor.

3

Integrative principles animate three of the most influential works that have dealt with French lyricism in the early seventeenth century. I refer, of course, to Odette de Mourgues's *Metaphysical, Baroque and Précieux Poetry,* Jean Rousset's *La Littérature de l'âge baroque en France,* and Imbrie Buffum's *Studies in the Baroque from Montaigne to Rotrou.*

Fundamentally a moralist, Odette de Mourgues refers literature to a preconstructional cause—artistic sensibility. This she divides into three aspects—intellect, imagination, and emotion—whose presence and hierarchy within the text furnish grounds for discriminating between types of poems and their relative merit. Much in the spirit of F. R. Leavis, Odette de Mourgues gives highest marks to the poetry of complete, coherent sensibility and downgrades works that lack even *one* of the components (or that contain *all* in a chaotic state). When applied to selected motifs, techniques, and stylistic devices of French poetry composed between the mid sixteenth century and the late seventeenth, Odette de Mourgues's model gives a place of honor to the metaphysical creations of Scève and La Ceppède, along with the *Adonis* of La Fontaine.[3] Far less esteemed are the brittle exercises of pure wit penned by the *précieux,* as well as the poetry of Saint-Amant, Théophile de Viau, and others, discussed under the heading "baroque." Her analysis of representative passages drawn from the last category points up both incompleteness and imbalance: in its visionary, absurd, and fragmented subject matter, its arational arrangement of materials, and its gratuitously playful, highly convoluted style.

Jean Rousset's critical scope transcends the boundary of the word. For him ballet, painting, and the lyric, as well as sculpture, tragicomedy, and architecture, are analogous, even interchangeable products of successive, radically different zeitgeists. Shared by all the arts of a given period are repertories of themes, technical devices, and stylistic procedures, each implying the others, as well as the Common (if somewhat remote) Cause. His *âge baroque* is a period of profound instability in all domains, especially the moral and the psychological. Accordingly, its arts portray movement, metamorphosis, and disguise; their manner is one of ostentatious, explosive force and calculated incompleteness; and their style is studded with gorgeous, polyvalent devices, the concetto being a kind of master trope in poetry. Carefully selected extracts from the works of Malherbe, Théophile de Viau, and Saint-Amant (among others) serve to document this thesis. Rousset admirably avoids reductionism, however, by stressing the uniqueness of each poet's *oeuvre*: the orotundity of Malherbe's, the apocalyptic *hantise* of Théophile's, and the free-wheeling fantasy of Saint-Amant's.

Imbrie Buffum also refers poetry to a succession of radically different zeitgeists; but unlike Jean Rousset, he sees the spirit generating baroque art and literature as a force of unity and coherence. Its basis is the Nicene Creed, which affirms: (1) an acceptance of God's organically unified creation, the external world, in all its richness (including the contrast between illusion and reality); (2) the importance of incarnation (e.g., the Word made Flesh), hence of metamorphosis; and (3) the meaningfulness of suffering—even in its most spectacularly horrible form, Christ's crucifixion—because of the ultimate triumph of truth. Buffum's sympathetic if fragmented reading of Saint-Amant's "libertine" poems discloses the presence of almost all eight baroque categories.

Nothing could be more dogmatic than to dismiss integrative criticism as irrelevant to the formal study of the early seventeenth-century French lyric. Beyond the invaluable service of relating the poems to their cultural matrix, the integrative critics have raised most of the questions that now preoccupy their more literal-minded counterparts. Indeed the principal themes of formal analysis in this specialty are, and will long remain, the nature of arational structures in the poetic corpus (first noted by Odette de Mourgues), the function of disguised elements of form and style (identified by Jean Rousset), and the dimensions of organic unity (intuited by Imbrie Buffum). Inevitably, however, when questions posed in one critical language are answered in another, the import and purport of key terms undergo important modifications, as the next pages will show.

A LITERALISM OF THE IMAGINATION

Differential criticism addresses the literary work fundamentally in its own nature, not by analogy (or with reference) to extrapoetic qualities, activities, or fields of inquiry. (When such disciplines as psychology, rhetoric, or iconology *must* be brought into the discussion, they play the ancillary role of elucidating isolated constituents of form.) The general categories of differential criticism are, of course, those of the work itself: end or purpose; object or form (i.e., action and its analogues); manner or techniques of representation; and means or language (diction, figures, prosody). Individual critics may choose to dwell—more or less exhaustively—on one or any combination of these categories, recognizing that incompleteness presents the danger of reductionism. So, too, may the critic discuss the chosen aspects atomistically—as constituents and devices—or synthetically—as factors in the work's unity. In the very brief survey to follow, I shall pass from the most nearly complete and synthetic studies to the narrowest and most atomistic.

Lowry Nelson's comparative essay *Baroque Lyric Poetry* examines two aspects of form as they occur in a variety of typical lyrics: first, the rhetorical situation—or the relationship between speaker and audience; and second, the time patterns, seen as contexts of stability, change, and repetition. From this it follows that Nelson focuses on the techniques of dramatic monologue and such stylistic devices as manipulated verb tenses, exclamations, questions, and asyndeton. In Nelson's system the end of the poem's form is unity, conceived in sequential terms—that is, as the product of evolving relationships between rhetorical numbers, tied to the passage from point to point along one or more temporal continua, whether narrative, conversational, or circular. In the longer lyrics of Saint-Amant, Théophile, and even Malherbe, Nelson perceives "a tendency to emphasize performing aspects: characterization of the speaker and gradual [evolution of his viewpoint]" in addition to a sense of relative and manipulatable time.[4]

Considerably less broad in scope than Nelson's study are those that have pointed to the relationship of motif and style as a basis for characterizing early seventeenth-century French lyricism. Typical are two essays collected in John C. Lapp's final volume, *The Brazen Tower*, and my 1972 monograph on Malherbe.[5] Lapp, having borrowed the notion of sunken imagery from a Columbia thesis by Henry Wells entitled *Poetic Imagery*, comments on passages of poems by La Fontaine and Tristan L'Hermite as he seeks to describe the interplay between veiled mythic references and elements of the speaker's mental or verbal activity. In *Higher, Hidden Order* I argued for a coherence arising from the synthesis of *topoi,* among other formal constituents, and the speaker's explicit and implied analogical reasonings—particularly when the latter involve allusion to myth or literature.

The narrowest and most atomistic studies have dealt *in vacuo* with devices of language. Of these, the most celebrated and useful is René Fromilhague's *Malherbe: Technique et création poétique,* which systematized our understanding of the poet's versification and thereby provided a basis for critical reexamination of his art, as well as its influence.[6] Equally rigorous, and almost as exhaustive, Fernand Hallyn's *Formes métaphoriques dans la poésie lyrique de l'âge baroque en France* is a linguistic taxonomy that leaves unanswered only certain questions raised in my own monograph—no doubt because allusive metaphors are not consistently expressed as blunt verbal analogies. John Pederson's thesis, *Images et figures dans la poésie française de l'âge baroque,* renders a similar service of classification, but on a poet-by-poet basis and with the results eclectically related to notions of period style developed by Wölfflin and his followers.

Pederson's eclecticism is not an isolated instance. The recent contributions of Susan Tiefenbrun and Francis L. Lawrence have opened a richly promising perspective where integrative methods, based on structuralism and semiology, clearly subserve the differential ends of formal description.[7]

SOME INDEPENDENT VARIABLES AND A MODUS OPERANDI

In this essay I shall explore a differential line of inquiry, probing representative lyric texts to ascertain whether or not they are unified and—if they prove to be—then how, and to what degree?[8] By unity I refer to the text's principle of singleness, completeness, and integration. I shall assume throughout the essay that there are at least four types of unity and that within a given work two or more may coexist if hierarchized—that is, if a clear distinction is drawn between the fundamental type and any others that are contributory.

By unity most critics understand *consecutive* unity, which results when parts of an action (or its analogue in the lyric) are ordered and articulated by a principle of rigorous sequence. One such principle is causality, according to whose laws circumstantial and psychological probabilities or moral necessities are established at the beginning of a lyric (or a large-scale plot), elaborated in the middle and fulfilled at the end. Another principle of rigorous sequence is discursive logic, which dictates that the conclusion of a syllogism come after the premises as well as "follow from" them; that the evidence of an induction precede the inferred generality; and that the referent of a metaphor appear before the analogue. The third principle is tradition or custom, which sets alphabetical, numerical, and ritual order as well as their imitations in literature.

There are also three types of *nonconsecutive* unity. The first of these is descriptive, arising when the parts of a work (an anatomy, for example) are selected to exhibit various aspects of a state or substance and are arranged as variations on a theme or by the principle of suggestion. The second type of nonconsecutive unity is iterative, attributable to a series of similar scenes or episodes, usually with different personages and little or no causal linkage among successive segments. Finally there is the didactic unity of allegory, exemplum, parable, or fable. Here every element of character, situation, or action is a deductive, inductive, or analogical proof of a thesis.

My first operation in both parts of this essay is to test each poem's explicit developmental structure for the presence or absence of unity in any of the senses just described. As Odette de Mourgues has already noted, however, most poems of this period will offer problems: indeterminate or unpredictable progression in some cases and rupture of consecutive movement in others.

Wherever narration, reasoning, or fulfillment of a conventional series is broken up, consecutive unity, of course, is forfeited. It does not follow, however, that the poem is ipso facto a worthless chaos. Nevertheless, it seems reasonable to wonder how one could test Imbrie Buffum's notion of organic unity in poems such as these. The answer lies, I believe, in extending the idea of lyric activity. As speech or scene independent of a larger cause-effect structure, the lyric represents states or processes in the speaker's character or thought. Among the thought processes, of course, are symboling and analogizing, both of which may be more or less explicit or complete. If less so, they may involve at least two devices: the scattering of related but partial and suggestive terms throughout the discourse or (in the case of metaphor only) the modeling of situation, character, or action on the motifs of pre-existent literary materials. By subsumption, such symbols and metaphors (which Jean Rousset might classify as a rhetoric of disguise) could well have a compensatory effect on the unity of a poem whose other lines of development have been disrupted.

As my second operation in the chapters of part 1, therefore, I shall test disrupted poems for the presence or absence of compensatory devices and—if any are found—I shall attempt to discover their precise impact on the poem's form. Dealing in part 2 with poems that, though indeterminate in progression, already possess iterative or descriptive unity, I shall perform the same test to ascertain if dispersed symbolism or implicit analogical activity adds a further dimension to their coherence.

A final note on organization. Within each part of this essay, I arrange the poems by *type* of developmental structure. Within each chapter I outline the characteristics of the structure and provide evidence for a broad contrast between its uses by mid- to late-sixteenth-century poets and those of the early seventeenth century. My Afterword synthesizes and draws tentative conclusions from that contrast. There is also an Appendix, which corrects my earlier study of the Malherbian ode in the light of the present findings.

1. Gustave Lanson, *Histoire de la littérature française,* p. 366.

2. The pluralistic categories employed in the discussion to follow are derived from R. S. Crane, "The Multiplicity of Critical Languages," in *The Languages of Criticism and the Structure of Poetry,* pp. 3–38, and Elder Olson, "An Outline of Poetic Theory," in his *On Value Judgments in the Arts and Other Essays,* pp. 268–74. Regrettably, Wayne C. Booth's *Critical Understanding: The Powers and Limits of Pluralism* (Chicago: University of Chicago Press, 1979) appeared too late for me to incorporate its invaluable findings into my "metacritical" framework. For a sound, up-to-date treatment of many points raised in the following discussion, see Robert Nicolich, "The Baroque Dilemma." This article supplements and in large measure supersedes René Wellek's studies of the baroque and its scholars in *Concepts of Criticism.* For a critique of the poetry-painting analogy, see my "Malherbe and the Mannerist Hypothesis."

3. A comparative study, the book also addresses the poetry of Sidney and Donne.

4. Lowry Nelson, *Baroque Lyric Poetry,* pp. 23, 154.

5. John C. Lapp, *The Brazen Tower,* pp. 58–76; David Lee Rubin, *Higher, Hidden Order.*

6. See C. K. Abraham, *Enfin Malherbe.*

7. Susan W. Tiefenbrun, "Mathurin Régnier's *Macette*"; Francis L. Lawrence, "Saint-Amant's 'L'Hyver des Alpes,' a Structural Analysis."

8. The position developed here represents an adaptation of concepts contained in several theoretical statements by Elder Olson—*Tragedy and the Theory of Drama,* especially pp. 41–48; "The Lyric," in his *On Value Judgments in the Arts and Other Essays,* pp. 212–19; and *The Poetry of Dylan Thomas*—as well as Bernard Weinberg's *The Limits of Symbolism* and Cleanth Brooks's *The Well Wrought Urn.* These notions have been conjoined with (and refined by) concepts borrowed from Barbara Herrnstein Smith's *Poetic Closure*; "A Topography of Allusion," an unpublished lecture by Allan H. Pasco; and, of course, the treatment of allusive metaphor in my *Higher, Hidden Order.*

PART ONE
BEYOND DISRUPTION

1

François de Malherbe
Priere pour le Roy allant en Limozin

Among the activities most conducive to sequential
unity in the lyric, none is more common than the reasoning
process itself. Poetry of the French Renaissance abounds with
specimens. Many of Du Bellay's *Regrets,* for instance, are con-
structed like the eighty-fifth, "Flatter un crediteur, pour son
terme allonger,"[1] in which unsavory details of social life in
modern Rome lead inductively to a disabused proposition about
the knowledge most worth having in that decadent milieu.
Sonnet 113 of *L'Olive,* best known as *L'Idée,* presents a deductive argument: if life *is* but a moment in a platonically conceived
eternity, then preoccupation with earthly things can yield no
cognitive or esthetic gratification; required instead is a spiritual
leap to the essences, qualities, and states that exist only *au plus
haut ciel.* Finally, *Les Antiquitez de Rome* are predominantly
analogical or based on the proportion A : B :: C : D. The twelfth
poem in the collection, "Telz que lon vid jadis les enfans de la
Terre," is typical, likening the ruined hills of Rome—once so
defiant of the gods—to the earth-born Giants, whose siege of
Olympus ended in catastrophic failure. The reasonings in the
three examples are valid: the conclusion of the inductive sonnet
is probable; that of the deduction "follows"; and the analogy
does not break down, at least within the confines of the text.
Moreover, there is neither disruption nor digression nor ex-

cursus. In other words, the activity of every poem in the group is single, complete, and integrated as it passes from beginning to end.

This pleasant state of affairs does not, of course, obtain in all French discursive poems of the mid sixteenth century. The exceptions, however, appear to constitute isolated failures rather than formal experiments, or the first signs of a shift toward a new poetic. One indication of this is the complete absence of compensatory devices in the disrupted poems. For example, Du Bellay's thirtieth *Antiquité* ("Comme le champ semé en verdure foisonne") presents an irreparably defective analogy: the barbarians who pillaged Rome are likened to a rustic who harvests wheat; but *unlike* the barbarians, the self-same rustic (or a "similar") must have had a part in the origin and development of what he was later to strip away. Certain of the *Regrets,* however, resemble the thirty-ninth ("J'ayme la liberté, et languis en service"), the sixty-eighth ("Je hay du Florentin l'usuriere avarice"), or the eighty-sixth ("Marcher d'un grave pas et d'un grave sourci"), in which a set of particulars leads to an overstated or irrelevant or merely weak conclusion unsalvaged by any "deeper structure." Finally, as Bernard Weinberg demonstrated, the original version of Du Bellay's deductive lyric, *Contre les Pétrarquistes,* is frequently interrupted by digressions and muddled by diffuse argumentation.[2] Again, no underlying pattern of form offsets this poem's lack of consecutive unity.

Indeed it was not until the late sixteenth or early seventeenth century that certain poets apparently discovered or invented an art of breaching discursive structures without loss of formal coherence. The compensatory element of that art consisted in using covert analogy to reunite—often in subtle and unexpected ways—the debris of their inductive, deductive, or analogical edifices. From the evidence at hand, moreover, this choice seems to have entailed substitution of descriptive, iterative, or didactic unity for the abandoned principle of sequence. Malherbe's prayer of 1605 is a paradigm case of this art.

Priere pour le Roy allant en Limozin

I   O Dieu, dont les Bontez de nos larmes touchees,
Ont aux vaines fureurs les armes arrachees,
Et rangé l'insolence aux piez de la raison,

Puis qu'à rien d'imparfaict ta loüange n'aspire,
Acheve ton ouvrage au bien de cét Empire,
6   Et nous rends l'embonpoint comme la guerison.

II   Nous sommes soubs un Roy si vaillant, et si sage,
Et qui si dignement a faict l'apprentissage,
De toutes les vertus propres à commander,
Qu'il semble que cét heur nous impose silence,
Et qu'asseurez par luy de toute violence,
12   Nous n'avons plus suject de te rien demander.

III   Certes quiconque a veu pleuvoir dessus nos testes
Les funestes esclats des plus grandes tempestes
Qu'exciterent jamais deux contraires partis,
Et n'en voit aujourd'huy nulle marque paroistre,
En ce miracle seul il peut assez cognoistre
18   Quelle force a la main qui nous a garantis.

IV   Mais quoy? de quelque soin qu'incessamment il veille,
Quelque gloire qu'il ait à nulle autre pareille,
Et quelque excez d'Amour qu'il porte à nostre bien:
Comme eschaperons-nous en des nuicts si profondes,
Parmy tant de rochers que luy cachent les ondes,
24   Si ton entendement ne gouverne le sien?

V   Un malheur inconnu glisse parmy les hommes,
Qui les rend ennemis du repos où nous sommes;
La pluspart de leurs voeux tendent au changement:
Et comme s'ils vivoient des miseres publiques,
Pour les renouveller ils font tant de pratiques,
30   Que qui n'a point de peur n'a point de jugement.

VI   En ce fascheux estat ce qui nous reconforte,
C'est que la bonne cause est tousjours la plus forte,
Et qu'un bras si puissant t'ayant pour son appuy,
Quand la rebellion plus qu'une Hydre feconde,
Auroit pour le combattre assemblé tout le Monde,
36   Tout le Monde assemblé s'enfuiroit devant luy.

VII   Conforme donc, Seigneur, ta grace à nos pensees.
Oste-nous ces objects, qui des choses passees
Ramenent à nos yeux le triste souvenir:
Et comme sa valeur, maistresse de l'orage,
A nous donner la paix a monstré son courage,
42   Fais luire sa prudence à nous l'entretenir.

VIII   Il n'a point son espoir au nombre des armees,
Estant bien asseuré que ces vaines fumees

N'adjoustent que de l'ombre à nos obscuritez.
L'aide qu'il veut avoir, c'est que tu le conseilles:
Si tu le fais, Seigneur, il fera des merveilles,
48   Et vaincra nos souhaits par nos prosperitez.

IX   Les fuittes des meschans, tant soient elles secrettes,
Quand il les poursuivra n'auront point de cachettes:
Aux lieux les plus profonds ils seront esclairez:
Il verra sans effect leur honte se produire,
Et rendra les desseins qu'ils feront pour luy nuire,
54   Aussi-tost confondus comme deliberez.

X   La rigueur de ses loix, apres tant de licence,
Redonnera le coeur à la foible innocence,
Que dedans la misere on faisoit envieillir:
A ceux qui l'oppressoient, il ostera l'audace:
Et sans distinction de richesse, ou de race,
60   Tous de peur de la peine auront peur de faillir.

XI   La terreur de son nom rendra nos villes fortes,
On n'en gardera plus ny les murs ny les portes,
Les veilles cesseront aux sommets de nos tours:
Le fer mieux employé cultivera la terre,
Et le peuple qui tremble aux frayeurs de la guerre,
66   Si ce n'est pour danser, n'aura plus de tambours.

XII   Loin des meurs de son siecle il bannira les vices,
L'oysive nonchalance, et les molles delices
Qui nous avoient portez jusqu'aux derniers hazarts:
Les vertus reviendront de palmes couronnees,
Et ses justes faveurs aux merites donnees
72   Feront ressusciter l'excellence des Arts.

XIII   La foy de ses ayeux, ton amour, et ta crainte,
Dont il porte dans l'Ame une eternelle emprainte,
D'actes de pieté ne pourront l'assouvir:
Il estendra ta gloire autant que sa puissance:
Et n'ayant rien si cher que ton obeyssance,
78   Où tu le fais regner il te fera servir.

XIV   Tu nous rendras alors nos douces Destinees:
Nous ne reverrons plus ces fascheuses annees,
Qui pour les plus heureux n'ont produit que des pleurs:
Toute sorte de biens comblera nos familles,
La moisson de nos champs lassera les faucilles,
84   Et les fruicts passeront la promesse des fleurs.

XV   La fin de tant d'ennuis dont nous fusmes la proye,
Nous ravira les sens de merveille, et de joye;
Et d'autant que le Monde est ainsi composé,
Qu'une bonne Fortune en craint une mauvaise,
Ton pouvoir absolu, pour conserver nostre aise,
90   Conservera celuy qui nous l'aura causé.

XVI   Quand un roy faineant, la vergongne des Princes,
Laissant à ses flateurs le soin de ses Provinces,
Entre les voluptez indignement s'endort,
Quoy que l'on dissimule on n'en fait point d'estime:
Et si la verité se peut dire sans crime,
96   C'est avecques plaisir qu'on survit à sa mort.

XVII   Mais ce Roy, des bons Roys l'eternel exemplaire,
Que de nostre salut est l'Ange tutelaire,
L'infaillible refuge, et l'asseuré secours,
Son extréme douceur ayant dompté l'envie,
De quels jours assez longs peut-il borner sa vie,
102   Que nostre affection ne les juge trop cours?

XVIII   Nous voyons les Esprits nez à la tyrannie,
Ennuyez de couver leur cruelle manie,
Tourner tous leurs Conseils à nostre affliction:
Et lisons clairement dedans leur conscience,
Que s'ils tiennent la bride à leur impatience,
108   Nous n'en sommes tenus qu'à sa protection.

XIX   Qu'il vive donc, Seigneur, et qu'il nous face vivre:
Que de toutes ces peurs nos ames il delivre:
Et rendant l'Univers de son heur estonné,
Adjouste chaque jour quelque nouvelle marque
Au nom qu'il s'est acquis du plus rare Monarque,
114   Que ta Bonté propice ait jamais couronné.

XX   Cependant son Dauphin d'une vitesse pronte
Des ans de sa jeunesse accomplira le conte:
Et suivant de l'honneur les aimables appas,
De faits si renommez ourdira son histoire,
Que ceux qui dedans l'ombre eternellement noire,
120   Ignorent le Soleil ne l'ignoreront pas.

XXI   Par sa fatale main qui vengera nos pertes,
L'Espagne pleurera ses Provinces desertes,
Ses Chasteaux abbatus, et ses champs déconfits,
Et si de nos discors l'infame vitupere,
A peu la desrober aux victoires du Pere,
126   Nous la verrons captive aux triomphes du Fils. [3]

THE DISLOCATED ARGUMENT

The prayer begins and ends with a group of interconnected deductive reasonings. It is in the middle—the frequently anthologized "Age of Gold" passage—that logic gives way to the repetitions that put the poem's unity into doubt.

After the invocation (v. 1), which establishes the circumstances—the wars of religion recently and justly ended with divine assistance—the speaker opens his argument with an enthymeme:

> Puis qu' à rien d'imparfaict ta loüange n'aspire,
> Acheve ton ouvrage au bien de cét Empire,
> Et nous rends l'embonpoint comme la guerison.

(Vv. 4–6)

The speaker takes for granted that God (who is doubly perfect, i.e., both complete and flawless) contemplates only such action as reflects His nature and thus adds to His greater glory. He has undertaken to benefit France, as the first three verses of the prayer clearly show, but the task is only half finished: though out of danger, the country is still not in the best of condition. To be absolutely consistent (indeed, to avoid betraying His own nature) God must, in both senses of the word, *perfect* His labor.

There follow two complex and specific amplifications of his argument, with particular emphasis on the second premise (what God has *begun* to do for France) and the conclusion (what He must do to perfect his enterprise). In the passages paralleling the second premise, he prepares for those paralleling the conclusion by accenting the innately human but divinely remediable deficiencies of Henri IV.

The first subsidiary argument (vv. 7–48) focuses on the king's moral and intellectual qualities. True, he is excellent: "si vaillant, et si sage" (v. 7). He possesses "toutes les vertus propres à commander" (v. 9): "force" (v. 18), "soin" (v. 19), "gloire" (v. 20), and —above all, perhaps—an "excez d'Amour qu'il porte à nostre bien" (v. 21). Proof of this is his success in ending the religious wars so as to protect the interests of the pious, peaceful and conservative classes with which the speaker implicitly identifies himself (in stanza III, for example). But Henri's human *sagesse* is insufficient—the world abounds with grave and subtle dangers: "Comme eschaperons-nous en des nuicts si pro-

fondes, / Parmy tant de rochers que luy cachent les ondes [?]"
(vv. 22–23). In particular, there are political radicals and agita-
tors who, like Biron, would perversely and selfishly rekindle the
civil wars (stanza V). There is, in the last analysis, no hope
unless God's "entendement" (v. 24) governs the king's, and
hence the speaker concludes with the following plea: "Fais luire
sa prudence à nous l'entretenir" (v. 42). With the intellectual
"appuy" (v. 33) of God's *conseils* (v. 46), nothing else is needed
and triumph is assured:

> Quand la rebellion plus qu'une Hydre feconde,
> Auroit pour le combattre assemblé tout le Monde,
> Tout le Monde assemblé s'enfuiroit devant luy.
>
> (Vv. 34–36)

The speaker ends this phase of the prayer with a broad resumptive conclusion: "Si tu le fais, Seigneur, il fera des merveilles, /
Et vaincra nos souhaits par nos prosperitez" (vv. 47–48). Be-
sides clinching the first subsidiary argument, these two verses
also generate a six-stanza digression (vv. 49–84), a parataxis or
set of variations,[4] on the theme of "merveilles."

The digression has several distinctive features. Every item, for
example, falls within the boundaries of a single stanza, with
anaphora serving to mark its beginning: the first hemistich of all
the *sizains* but one opens with the formula of definite article /
noun / *des* or *de* plus possessive adjective / noun. The exception (v. 67) deviates from this pattern with adverb / *des* / noun in
the first *coupe*. But the *l* of *Loin* echoes those of the initial *les* and
la before and after. Within each item the progression is invariable, a movement from cause to effect. The speaker first reveals
the action the divinely aided Henri IV will take or the conditions
he will establish, then the anticipated results. Accordingly, in
stanza IX the king will apprehend the wicked who, consequently, will be foiled and disgraced. In X he will enact severe
laws that will encourage the innocent and intimidate the oppres-
sive. In XI his reputation alone will fortify cities, so that swords
will be beaten into ploughshares and drums will furnish rhythms
for dancing, not marching. Stanza XII predicts Henri's abolition
of vice: merit and art will gain from this. In XIII he will restore
traditional religious observances: worship of God will therefore
spread wherever Henri rules. It is crucial that no item in this

catalogue is the logical or causal precondition to—or effect of—any other. Everything is foreseen as occurring more or less simultaneously and in consequence of God's expected aid to a supremely virtuous sovereign.

To conclude this digression, the speaker departs from the pattern he has established: anaphora does not appear after verse 78; stanza XIV opens with a direct address to God, "Tu nous rendras alors nos douces Destinees" (v. 79); and generated by this verse, a resumptive list of benefits replaces cause-effect alternation in the rest of the finale. Evil times will not return and

> Toute sorte de biens comblera nos familles,
> La moisson de nos champs lassera les faucilles,
> Et les fruicts passeront la promesse des fleurs.
>
> (Vv. 82–84)

The final lines close a circle, with a return to the beginning of the digression for the idea of overwhelming "prosperitez" (v. 48).

Forming a bridge between the digression and the second deductive movement is a contrast between the people's future joy and fear:

> La fin de tant d'ennuis dont nous fusmes la proye,
> Nous ravira les sens de merveille, et de joye,
> Et d'autant que le Monde est ainsi composé
> Qu'une bonne Fortune en craint une mauvaise.
>
> (Vv. 85–88)

Specifically, Henri IV is blemished by mortality. Though no fault at all in a degenerate (like Henri III; cf. stanza XVI), in France's "Ange tutelaire" (v. 98) it necessarily portends disaster, for:

> Nous voyons les Esprits nez à la tyrannie,
> Ennuyez de couver leur cruelle manie,
> Tourner tous leurs Conseils à nostre affliction.
>
> (Vv. 103–5)

Obviously it would be counterproductive to ask God to complete His work in France's favor by making Henri IV immortal, and so the speaker hopes for something less, something feasible: that God's "pouvoir absolu, pour conserver nostre aise, / Conservera celuy qui nous l'aura causé" (vv. 89–90). Thus the first part of the conclusion makes the plea, "Qu'il vive donc, Seigneur, et qu'il nous face vivre" (v. 109). The second part follows from the first. As Henri must eventually die, the completion and preservation of his work depends on a completely reliable successor—if possible, a replica:

> Cependant son Dauphin d'une vitesse pronte
> Des ans de sa jeunesse accomplira le conte:
> . . . .
> Par sa fatale main qui vengera nos pertes,
> L'Espagne pleurera ses Provinces desertes,
> . . . .
> Et si de nos discors l'infame vitupere,
> A peu la desrober aux victoires du Pere,
> Nous la verrons captive aux triomphes du Fils
>
> (Vv. 115–16, 121–22, 124–26)

With the king's deficiencies remedied to the fullest possible extent, the deductive movement closes on a strong note of finality and definition. The arrested expectation of further development is reinforced by a shift of syntax: the second part of the conclusion appears, not as a plea, but as a simple assertion of futurity.

In itself, the deductive portion of the prayer is not only single in form but complete and integrated. In itself, the parataxis attains a high degree of internal coherence as well. Placed together, however, they work at cross purposes, as one tends toward consecutive unity and the other toward a more descriptive harmony. As the two yoked structures strain in different directions, the prayer seems doomed to fly apart. Yet it does not.

FIGURES AND TYPES

Clues to the unifying pattern of the prayer appear in Malherbe's paraphrase of snippets from at least two ancient texts. Such transposition always invites systematic comparison of motifs, and in this case the effort discloses that in part the later poem is modeled on the earlier two, and that implicit analogies exist between the various protagonists, events, and settings.

Psalm 72

Three verses of Malherbe's prayer echo four of this psalm, generally interpreted as David's petition to God for the success of Solomon's reign:[5]

> He shall give judgment for the suffering,
> and help those of the people that are needy:
> He shall crush the oppressor. . . .
>
> (V. 4)[6]

For he shall rescue the needy from their rich
oppressors, the distressed who have no protector,
May he have pity on the needy and the poor,
deliver the poor from death:
may he redeem them from oppression and violence
and may their blood be precious in his
eyes. . . .

(Vv. 12–14)

La rigueur de ses loix, apres tant de licence,
Redonnera le coeur à la foible innocence,
Que dedans la misere on faisoit envieillir:
A ceux qui l'oppressoient, il ostera l'audace . . .

(Vv. 55–58)

Resemblances between the psalm and the prayer do not, of course, end here. In fact, materials from almost half of the former recur in the latter. Because of their similarity to verses 4 and 12–14 of the psalm, for example, verses 1 and 2—

O God, endow the king with thy own justice,
give thy righteousness to a king's son,
that he may judge thy people rightly and
deal out justice to the poor and suffering . . .

—are analogous to the key lines of Malherbe's tenth stanza, quoted above. Verses 7 and 16 of the psalm focus on righteousness and abundance:

In his days righteousness shall flourish,
prosperity abound until the moon is no
more . . .

May there be abundance of corn in the land,
growing in plenty to the tops of the hills;
may the crops flourish like Lebanon,
and the sheaves be numberless as blades of
grass.

These lines are coextensive with portions of stanzas VIII, XII, and XIV of Malherbe:

Et vaincra nos souhaits par nos prosperitez.
. . . .
Loin des meurs de son siecle bannira les vices,
L'oysive nonchalance, et les molles delices
. . . .

> Toute sorte de biens comblera nos familles,
> La moisson de nos champs lassera les faucilles,
> Et les fruicts passeront la promesse de fleurs.
>
> (Vv. 48, 67–68, 82–84)

The literal and symbolic humiliation of enemies is the thematic link between verse 9 of the psalm and stanza XXI of Malherbe's prayer:

> Ethiopians shall crouch low before him:
>   his enemies shall lick the dust.
>
> L'Espagne pleurera . . .
> Ses Chasteaux *abbatus*. . . .
>
> (Vv. 122–23, emphasis added)

In both cases, prestige compels deference: " . . . all kings shall pay him homage" (v. 11) while Henri IV possesses the name "du plus rare Monarque, / Que ta Bonté propice ait jamais couronné" (vv. 113–14), and the Dauphin,

> . . . suivant de l'honneur les aimables appas,
> De faits si renommez ourdira son histoire,
> Que ceux qui dedans l'ombre eternellement noire,
> Ignorent le Soleil ne l'ignoreront pas.
>
> (Vv. 117–20)

Finally, added to universal celebrity, there is the topos of everlasting fame:

> Long may the king's name endure,
> may it live forever like the sun,
> so shall all peoples pray to be blessed as he was,
> all nations tell of his happiness.
>
> (V. 17)

For his part, Henri IV will be "des bons Roys l'eternel exemplaire" (v. 97).

The frequent echoes of Psalm 72 in both the deductive and paratactic passages of Malherbe's prayer implicate the entire poem in an analogy of the following sort:

> Solomon : Israel :: Henri IV : France

If certain key continua cannot be missed—e.g., the king as savior of his country as well as future cause of moral and legal regeneration, material well-being, and triumph over adversaries—there is an equally important point of similarity that is far less obvious: that France, like Israel, is (or should be) God's most favored nation. But the analogy also presents some negative parallels, points of significant difference between the Solomon of Psalm 72 and the Henri IV of Malherbe's prayer. First, the French king has ended a civil war, resumption of which is a constant threat. Solomon will confront no such challenge, if David's prayer is answered, and accordingly, his task will be lighter, his accomplishments less impressive. Second, Malherbe credits Henri IV with military virtues that the psalm does not attribute to Solomon, even indirectly. Third David portrays the future king as an imperialist: "May he hold sway from sea to sea, from the River to the ends of the earth"(v. 8). By contrast, Henri IV has the juster and more modest goal of securing French frontiers by neutralizing Spain (stanza XXI). Fourth, the psalm contains no mention of Solomon's eventual successor, the continuator of his policies, whereas Malherbe provides for dynastic succession in the person of the Dauphin.

All in all, it is not Henri IV as a modern Solomon that Malherbe implicitly portrays, but Henri IV as a less flawed, more fully realized version of the Solomon prototype set forth in the psalm. A paragon of all the virtues possessed and lacked by the future Hebrew king, he will face and, God willing, surmount greater challenges than those David foresaw for his own son.

As rhetoric primarily intended for the approval of the king, the function of the qualified analogy requires no comment. As rhetoric addressed to God, however, it does. In the deductive sections of the prayer, the speaker's entire argument reposes on a belief that God has been slow to act in France's favor and so has withheld the *merveilles* foreseen in the digression. The analogy thus constitutes an *a fortiori* appeal: if God in any degree favored Israel and the house of David, how can He do less for a nation and a royal line that (given the speaker's evidence and reasonings) are similar but more deserving, because actually and potentially they are greater in the same ways? Again, the argument is from consistency, a necessary attribute of God, who is perfect and aims at nothing less than perfection.

Eclogue IV

In eclogue IV, the most famous of Virgil's ten bucolic poems, the speaker addresses the consul Pollio, predicting that the Golden Age will return during his period in office and that both will coincide with the birth of a particularly gifted and privileged child, perhaps the consul's own son. Several verses of the Latin poem sonorously echo in Malherbe's prayer:[7]

> . . . and you can know what valor is . . .
>
> (V. 27)[8]

> . . . il peut assez cognoistre
> Quelle force a la main qui nous a garantis.
>
> (Vv. 17–18)

> . . . to gird towns with walls and to cleave the earth with furrows . . .
>
> (Vv. 32–33)

> On n'en gardera plus ny les murs ny les portes,
> . . . .
> Le fer mieux employé cultivera la terre.
>
> (Vv. 62, 64)[9]

> . . . slowly shall the plain yellow with waving corn . . .
>
> (V. 28)

> La moisson de nos champs lassera les faucilles.
>
> (V. 83)

Complementing these verbal parallels are numerous similarities of motif, including some that blend with the biblical materials discussed in the preceding section. The parallel motifs include the return of justice:

> Now the Virgin (i.e., Astraea) returns . . .
>
> (V. 6)

> La rigueur de ses loix, apres tant de licence,
> Redonnera le coeur à la foible innocence,
> Que dedans la misere on faisoit envieillir:
> A ceux qui l'oppressoient, il ostera l'audace:
>
> (Vv. 55–58);

the return of traditional religious observances:

> . . . the reign of Saturn returns . . .
>
> (V. 6)

> La foy de ses ayeux, ton amour, et ta crainte,
> Dont il porte dans l'Ame une eternelle emprainte,
> D'actes de pieté ne pourront l'assouvir
>
> (Vv. 73–75);

the beginning of a new age that coincides with the administration of a great political leader:

> And in your consulship, Pollio, shall this
> glorious age begin, and the mighty months
> commence their march . . .
>
> (Vv. 11–12)

> Nous sommes soubs un Roy si vaillant, et si sage,
> Et qui si dignement a faict l'apprentissage,
> De toutes les vertus propres à commander
>
> (Vv. 7–9);

the association of the leader's progeny with the new age: stanzas XIX and XX of the ode and

> . . . the child under whom the iron race shall
> first cease and a golden race spring up
> throughout the world . . .
>
> (Vv. 8–9 and passim thereafter);

fertility and prosperity resulting from the new order:

> . . . the earth untilled shall pour forth, as her
> first pretty gifts, straggling ivy with foxglove
> everywhere, and the Egyptian bean blended with
> the smiling acanthus. Uncalled, the goats shall
> bring home their udders swollen with milk . . .
>
> (Vv. 18–22)

> Assyrian spice shall spring up on every soil . . .
>
> (V. 25)

> . . . slowly shall the plain yellow with the
> waving corn, on wild brambles shall hang the
> purple grape, and the stubborn oak shall distill
> dewy honey . . .
>
> (Vv. 28–30)

> Et vaincra nos souhaits par nos prosperitez.
>
> (V. 48)

> Toute sorte de biens comblera nos familles,
> La moisson de nos champs lassera les faucilles,
> Et les fruicts passeront la promesse des fleurs.
>
> (Vv. 82–84);

the identification of serpents and evil:

> The serpent, too, shall perish . . .
>
> (V. 24)

> Un malheur inconnu glisse parmy les hommes,
> Qui les rend ennemis du repos où nous sommes
>
> (Vv. 25–26);

and finally, the persistence of sin and war:

> Yet a few traces of past sin shall lurk behind
>
> (V. 31)

> Nous voyons les Esprits nez à la tyrannie,
> Ennuyez de couver leur cruelle manie,
> Tourner tous leurs Conseils à nostre affliction:
> Et lisons clairement dedans leur conscience,
> Que s'ils tiennent la bride à leur impatience,
> Nous n'en sommes tenus qu'à sa protection.
>
> (Vv. 103–8)

Implicit in the foregoing, and subsuming both the deductive and the paratactic passages, is an analogy on the following order: Pollio and the child : Rome : the Age of Gold :: Henri IV and the Dauphin : France : the age of "merveilles"[10] No redundancy, this allusive metaphor contributes important new elements to the prayer's structure. By its presentation of a profane counterpart of the first allusion, it of course provides thematic symmetry and a sense of the universal. More important, however, is the augmented grandeur—cultural, political, and even physical—indirectly attributed to France by comparison with Rome. Finally, the Virgilian allusion accents the idea, dear to Malherbe, of a new order about to establish itself, in contrast with the expectation of mere improvement in social and material circumstances announced in the psalm. Some of the elements contributed by this analogy, however, are oxymoronic.[11] Neither Pollio nor the child is personally responsible for the return of the Golden Age. Fate had already decreed the cyclical change during the consul's term, or so Virgil's speaker hopes: "Now is come the last age of the song of Cumae; / the great line of the centuries begins anew'' (vv. 4–5). The consul is merely a contemporary of the events and the child ranks as its symbol and great beneficiary. By contrast, it is Henri IV himself, aided by God's gifts of advice, longevity, and a successor in his own image, who will radically alter the life of France. Therefore father (and son) will deserve the credit that the prayer grants in advance. Second, the Age of Gold predicted by Virgil[12] initiates a circuit that must necessarily end with a savage race of iron. Malherbe's prayer, by contrast, opens a perspective on the possibility of limitless peace and abundance. The perfection of God's work ''au bien de cét Empire'' implies nothing less.

FORM AND IDEOLOGY

From this analysis it is clear that the prayer possesses iterative unity: the warring developmental contexts resolve themselves into a literal statement of the formula echoed (however roughly) by the allusive metaphors. Underpinning the whole structure—the logic, the repetitions, the analogies, and the rhetorical end they subserve—is a peculiar view of the historical process. Obviously, the cyclical theory figures here in some form, but, from the qualifications set on the analogies and the conditional character of certain propositions, explicit and implied, it is equally obvious that the poem does not repose on the idea of mechanically repeated complexes of men and events. Rather, a distinction exists between two broad types of cyclical recurrence. In one, the complex remains pure potentiality: there is no great shift in politics, morals, economics, or law, because the supernatural power capable of effectuating such a shift does not intervene. Thus many of David's hopes as well as the predictions of Virgil are unfulfilled: Solomon fails to raise his people's standard of living and eventually yields to greed and impiety (I Kings 9–12); Rome does not see the return of the Golden Age during the consulship of Pollio (or anyone else); and the Jewish Messiah is still awaited. History, in short, undergoes no divine manipulation. In the second type of cyclical recurrence, the realization of a complex at least begins because a supernatural force *does* intervene. Within this framework of manipulated history, the protagonist may equal or in some measure surpass his prototypes by assuming or perfecting their virtues and consolidating them with his own as a basis for action, while shedding his defects and acquiring none of theirs. Finally, whether or not the divinity permits complete realization of the complex, the favored nation will flourish and the protagonist will necessarily become a model for human excellence, thus adding to the glory of the divine patron.[13]

Diffuse or disrupted argumentation—counterbalanced by implicit analogy or dispersed symbolism—appears in many French poems of this period, including Régnier's *Macette,* Saint-Amant's "Entrer dans un $\beta o \rho \delta \epsilon \lambda$," Théophile de Viau's *Elegie à une dame,* Maynard's *La Belle Vieille,*[14] and Tristan L'Hermite's *Promenoir des deux amans,*"[15] as well as all of Abraham de Vermeil's discursive sonnets.[16]

1. All citations of Du Bellay are from Albert-Marie Schmidt, ed., *Poètes du 16e siècle.*

2. Bernard Weinberg, "Du Bellay's 'Contre les Pétrarquistes.'"

3. All citations of the prayer are from François de Malherbe, *Oeuvres poétiques,* 1:58–62.

4. See chapter 5, below, for a fuller discussion of paratactic structure.

5. Malherbe, 2:15.

6. All scriptural citations are from *The New English Bible,* pp. 671–72.

7. Malherbe, 2:15–16.

8. All citations of the eclogue are based on the revised edition of *Virgil I,* edited and translated by H. R. Fairclough, pp. 28–33.

9. Vv. 62 and 64 of the Malherbe echo Isaiah 2:4, which predicts a messianic age:

> he will be judge between nations,
> arbiter among many peoples.
> They shall beat their swords into mattocks
> and their spears into pruning knives;
> nation shall not lift sword against nation
> nor ever again be trained for war.
> (*The New English Bible,* pp. 810–11)

This would imply a subsidiary analogy between Henri IV and Israel's Savior God, while illustrating once again Malherbe's technique of blending allusions (see vv. 55–58).

10. Also suggested is the similarity between Malherbe('s persona) and Virgil('s), and hence David('s). For a discussion of this possibility in Malherbe's last ode, see Judd D. Hubert, "Myth and Status."

11. The notion of oxymoronic or negative function in implicit metaphor was developed by Allan H. Pasco in "A Topography of Allusion," a lecture delivered at the University of Virginia on 4 November 1974.

12. And Isaiah, see note 9.

13. Though Malherbe's sources were—and in some quarters still *are*—interpreted as prophecies of Jesus Christ, it would be difficult to argue that the prayer establishes a parallel between the King of France and the Son of God. To be sure, Henri IV *is* represented as a restorer of peace and proper values, but his field of action is fundamentally political, his means often intimidating, and his nature fallibly human. It is the purpose of the prayer to elicit correction of his main shortcomings so that he might surpass those who prefigured Christ, rather than equal the Messiah in character or powers.

14. See Susan Tiefenbrun's semiological analysis of this text, "*La Belle Vieille* de François Maynard."

15. See Wolfgang Leiner, "'Le Promenoir des deux amans,' lecture d'un poème de Tristan L'Hermite."

16. See Abraham de Vermeil, *Poésies,* and my article "Mannerism and Love."

2

Saint-Amant
Le Mauvais Logement

As frequent as logic in the consecutive lyric is an order based on time or causality. The work of Ronsard is particularly rich in examples, exhibiting not only a broad spectrum of forms and functions but also the problems of unity that may arise in the loosest type of "temporal-causal structure."[1]

Anecdotal or descriptive material may, of course, serve very different purposes.[2] At the very least, it may furnish a pretext for moral choices, affective activity, or reasonings, expressed in dramatic or interior monologue, or in colloquy. In the seventeenth of Ronsard's *Amours diverses,* for example, the speaker devotes the first quatrain to a narration-cum-description, laden with paradoxical significance:

> Je liay d'un filet de soye cramoisie
> Vostre bras l'autre jour, parlant avecques vous:
> Mais le bras seulement fut captif de mes nouds,
> Sans vous pouvoir lier ny coeur ny fantaisie.
>
> (Vv. 1–4)[3]

The remaining verses present the speaker's impossible wishes and melancholy sentiments occasioned by musing on that significance:

> Beauté, que pour maistresse unique j'ay choisie,
> Le sort est inegal: vous triomphez de nous.

> Vous me tenez esclave esprit, bras, & genous,
> Et Amour ne vous tient ny prinse ny saisie.
>
> Je veux parler, Maistresse, à quelque vieil sorcier,
> A fin qu'il puisse au mien vostre vouloir lier,
> Et qu'une mesme playe à noz coeurs soit semblable.
>
> Je faux: l'amour qu'on charme, est de peu de sejour.
> Estre beau, jeune, riche, eloquent, agreable,
> Non les vers enchantez, sont les sorciers d'Amour.
>
> (Vv. 5–14)

Situations, character, or action may also be elements of proof in an argument, as in the celebrated sonnet "Quand vous serez bien vieille, au soir à la chandelle."[4] Here the speaker paradoxically foresees himself as happy, even vital, though a *fantaume sans os,* and Hélène—having refused his suit—as the very image of inconsolable death-in-life. All of this materially supports the speaker's fundamental thesis that Hélène should "seize the day." Finally, story elements may have no literal function at all; instead they may constitute symbols of inner states or processes. Consider, for example, the second of Ronsard's *Sonnets pour Hélène* I, "Quand à longs traits je boy l'amoureuse estincelle," where the anecdote of poisoning and bedazzlement by the lady's eyes translates the speaker's tumultuous inner reaction to the spectacle of Hélène's beauty.[5]

Structurally, the temporal-causal lyric may fall into one of three categories. The nineteenth ode in Ronsard's second book is "framed," relating the unseemly behavior of Amor, who—rainsoaked—seeks shelter with the speaker and then "me tire une fleche amere / Droict en l'oeil" (vv. 52–53).[6] There follows a commentary that draws a more or less logical conclusion from the complete symbolic anecdote:

> Voila, Robertet, le bien,
> (Mon Robertet qui embrasses
> L'heur des Muses, & des Graces)
> Le bien qui m'est survenu
> Pour loger un incognu.
>
> (Vv. 58–62)

But the narrative may be "unframed" as well, relating a complete incident without terminal (or prefatory) comment, often because of the metaphor- or symbol-laden character of the matter, as the poet treats it. Ronsard's eighty-ninth *Amour*, "Soubz le cristal d'une argenteuse rive," exemplifies the type, narrating the speaker's discovery of the perfect pearl (which represents ideal feminine beauty) and his unsuccessful attempts to fish it out of an equally nonliteral stream.[7] For my purposes, however, the most interesting kind of temporal-causal structure is neither the framed nor the unframed narrative, but rather "simultaneous composition." Here, a situation or an isolated action is presented and followed immediately by an amplified response—moral, affective, or intellectual.[8] The pattern may recur any number of times in a given lyric so that, finally, a complex situation or event may be presented in its fullness, but the manner is invariably piecemeal, never continuous.

The seventeenth of Ronsard's first book of sonnets to Hélène is characteristic, presenting two narrative-reactive units. The first of these concerns the speaker's view of the two women together: "Te regardant assise aupres de ta cousine" (v. 1),[9] and then relates his effusive, hyperbolic reaction: "Belle comme une Aurore, & toy comme un Soleil, / Je pensay voir deux fleurs d'un mesme teint pareil" (vv. 2–3). The second presents the contrast between the glances returned by Hélène and her cousin:

La chaste, saincte, belle & unique Angevine,
Viste comme un esclair, sur moy jetta son oeil:
Toy comme paresseuse, & pleine de sommeil,
D'un seul petit regard tu ne m'estimas digne.

Tu t'entretenois seule au visage abaissé,
Pensive toute à toy, n'aimant rien que toymesme,
Desdaignant un chascun d'un sourcil ramassé,

Comme une qui ne veut qu'on la cherche ou qu'on l'aime . . .
(Vv. 5–12)

His reaction follows: "J'euz peur de ton silence, & m'en-allay tout blesme, / Craignant que mon salut n'eust ton oeil offensé" (v. 13–14). Although this sonnet is single, complete, and integrated, simultaneous composition in fact lends itself, more than any other temporal-causal mode, to *dis*unity. Two other poems by Ronsard illustrate the problem.

Dedans des Prez je vis une Dryade,
Qui comme fleur s'assisoyt par les fleurs,

Et mignotoyt un chappeau de couleurs,
Eschevelée en simple verdugade.

Des ce jour là ma raison fut malade,
Mon cuoeur pensif, mes yeulx chargez de pleurs,
Moy triste et lent: tel amas de douleurs
En ma franchise imprima son oeillade.

Là je senty dedans mes yeulx voller
Un doulx venin, qui se vint escouler
Au fond de l'ame: & depuis cest oultrage,

Comme un beau lis, au moys de Juin blessé
D'un ray trop chault, languist à chef baissé
Je me consume au plus verd de mon age.[10]

Here the cause-effect order is pointlessly scrambled, with immediate consequences (vv. 9–11) placed between others that are long-range (vv. 5–8 and 12–14), although the former are necessary antecedents to the latter. In the next case, the effects are exhibited at random:

Quand je vous voi, ou quand je pense en vous,
Je ne sçai quoi dans le coeur me fretille,
Qui me pointelle, & tout d'un coup me pille
L'esprit emblé d'un ravissement dous.

Je tremble tout de nerfs & de genous:
Comme la cire au feu, je me distile,
Sous mes souspirs: & ma force inutile
Me laisse froid, sans haleine & sans pous.

Je semble au mort, qu'on devale en la fosse,
Ou à celui qui d'une fievre grosse
Perd le cerveau, dont les esprits mués

Révent cela, qui plus leur est contraire.
Ainsi, mourant, je ne sçauroi tant faire,
Que je ne pense en vous, qui me tués.[11]

No principle except, perhaps, that of repetition accounts for the presence of reactive elements or their "order of telling." In neither case, moreover, does a submerged analogical reasoning (or any other compensatory device) pull the *disjecta membra* into a nonconsecutive whole.[12]

In Saint-Amant's caprice *La Mauvais Logement,* all of these disruptive elements appear, along with another, peculiar to longer poems of this kind, namely, the atomization of external experience and the breakdown of all sense of time.

Le Mauvais Logement

Gisté dans un chien de grabat,
Sur un infame lit de plume,
Entre deux draps teins d'apostume,
Où la Vermine me combat:
5   Je passe les plus tristes heures
Qui dans les mortelles Demeures
Puissent affliger les Esprits;
Et la Nuit si longue m'y semble,
Que je croy qu'elle ait entrepris
10 D'en joindre une douzaine ensemble.

Parmy tant d'incommoditez
Je conte tous les coups de Cloche;
Et comme un Oyson à la broche
Je me tourne de tous costez:
15 Une vilaine Couverture,
Relique de la pourriture,
Malgré moy s'offre à me baiser;
Mais, si je luy deffens ma bouche,
Je ne sçaurois luy refuser
20 Qu'à mes jambes elle ne touche.

Elle suplante les linceuls
Qui se sauvent dans la ruelle;
Mais pour fuïr cette crüelle
Les pauvrets n'y vont pas tous seuls:
25 Un Manteau de laine d'Espagne
En ce chemin les accompagne,
Du travail à demy suant,
Et sans prétendre à la victoire,
Dans un pot de chambre puant
30 Il glisse, et va chercher à boire.

Au clair de la Lune qui luit
D'une lueur morne, et blafarde,
Mon oeil tout effrayé regarde
Voltiger mille oyseaux de Nuit:
35 Les Chauvesouris, les Fresayes
Dont les cris sont autant de playes
A l'oreille qui les entend,
Decoupans l'Air humide et sombre,
Percent jusqu'où mon corps s'estend,
40 Et le muguettent comme une ombre.

Un essaim de maudits Cousins,
Bruyant d'une fureur extresme,

Me fait renasquer en moy-mesme
Contre la saison des raisins:
45 L'un sur ma main donne en Sang-suë;
L'autre sur ma trongne se ruë,
Me rendant presque tout méseau;
Je les poursuy, je les attrappe,
Et sans m'épargner le museau
50 Pour les y tuër je me frappe.

Cent Rats, d'insolence animez,
Se querellent sous une table
Où jamais repas délectable
N'apparut aux yeux affamez:
55 Là tantost aux barres ils joüent;
Là tantost ils s'entre-secoüent,
Pipans d'un ton aigre et mutin;
Et tantost cette fauce race
S'en vient ronger pour tout festin
60 Les entrailles de ma paillace.

Une trouppe de Farfadets
Differens de taille, et de forme,
L'un ridicule, et l'autre énorme,
S'y deméne en Diables-Cadets:
65 Ma viziere en est fascinée,
Mon oüye en est subornée,
Ma cervelle en est hors de soy;
Bref, ces fabriqueurs d'impostures
Estalent tout autour de moy
70 Leurs grimaces, et leurs postures.

Les Rideaux ne m'empeschent point
De voir toutes leurs singeries;
Ces infernales nigeries
Me font fremir sous l'embonpoint:
75 J'ay beau pour en perdre l'image
Qui me baille un teint de fromage
M'efforcer à cligner les yeux,
L'effroy me taillant des croupieres,
Par un effet malicieux
80 Change en bezicles mes paupieres.

Maints faux rayons éparpillez
En fanfreluches lumineuses,
Offrent cent chimeres hideuses
A mes regars en vain sillez:

85   Ma trop credule fantaisie
      En est si vivement saisie
      Qu'elle mesme se fait horreur;
      Et sentant comme elle se pâme,
      Je me figure en cette erreur
90   Qu'on donne le moine à mon ame.

       Que si je pense m'endormir,
      Dans les momens de quelque tréve,
      Un Incube aussi tost me créve,
      Et resvant je m'entr'oy gémir.
95   En fin mes propres cris m'éveillent,
      En fin ces Demons s'émerveillent
      D'estre quasi surpris du jour;
      Ils font gille à son arrivée,
      Et la diane du tambour
100   M'avertit que l'Aube est levée.[13]

In this interior monologue the speaker (who is either a soldier in or hanger-on of an active military detachment) relates his conflict with the grotesque inhabitants of a commandeered inn where he is quartered. At first disgusted, then frightened and confused, he passes through a series of real and imagined horrors culminating in a nightmare of homosexual rape. Then, at long last, dawn disperses his assailants and reveille sounds.

The first fourteen verses follow the usual pattern of simultaneous composition: the speaker more or less emotionally describes his circumstances and narrates what befalls him; then he exhibits an amplified but not less immediate reaction. For hours he is "gisté" (v. 1) on a contemptible bed, covered by a foul "lit de plume" (v. 2), using sheets colored by the effluvia of an unfortunate predecessor (v. 3). Most importantly, he is attacked by "la Vermine" (v. 4). As a result of all this, he experiences not only pain and malaise without equal, especially given his location (vv. 5–6), but a decreasing awareness of temporal flow, joined with a growing sense of persecution:

    Et la Nuit si longue m'y semble,
    Que je croy qu'elle ait entrepris
    D'en joindre une douzaine ensemble.

              (Vv. 8–10)

This is no idle exaggeration: indeed, it makes probable a later shift in the speaker's mental activity, from straight narration-cum-reaction to delusion, entailing a total breakdown of temporal-causal perception and an almost overwhelming paranoia. Now, however, the speaker repeats the pattern of verses 1–10, beginning to list the "incommoditez" (v. 11) to which he is subject. The first of these is all but predictable, considering his preoccupation with time: "Je conte tous les coups de Cloche" (v. 12). He then succumbs to agitation: "Et comme un Oyson à la broche, / Je tourne de tous costez" (vv. 13–14). Because *et* is ambiguous, the reader cannot know how the speaker perceives this change of condition: is it coextensive with the steady, lugubrious pealing of the bell, or does it ensue upon the sound, or is it a mere supervention? This ambiguity, however, is functional: it clears the way for the second part of the caprice, which opens with a hallucination, no doubt the result of the totality of his sufferings.

Tossing and turning, the speaker disarranges his covers so thoroughly that one of them rises to his mouth, while the *linceuls*—along with the *Manteau de laine d'Espagne*—fall off the bed completely, the latter sliding into a *pot de chambre puant*. Obviously, though, the event is not so perceived: no causal detail links verse 14 with 15 and 16: "Je me tourne de tous costez: / Une vilaine Couverture." Moreover, all but one of the inanimate objects involved here are personified. The *Couverture* is not only sordid, but *malhonnête*. The speaker perceives it as so maddened by desire that when its more sedate approaches receive no encouragement, it becomes emboldened to take other liberties:

> Malgré moy [elle] s'offre à me baiser;
> Mais, si je luy deffens ma bouche,
> Je ne sçaurois luy refuser
> Qu'à mes jambes elle ne touche.

> (Vv. 17–20)

In the process, the *Couverture* is seen supplanting the bed's other accouterments, no doubt because they appear to be rivals who have succeeded (without effort) in closing in on the speaker's appetizing body. Of the *Couverture*'s victims, the *Manteau* is imagined as so pathetically exercised that it suffers from dehydration and slithers into the *pot de chambre* to slake its thirst.

The emotional and imaginative paroxysm related in the first hallucination now closes, and the speaker returns to an alternance of affective narration or description followed by an immediate, amplified response. Without temporal or causal transition, he shifts to the *clair de lune* (v. 31), on which he projects his own mood, seeing it shine "d'une lueur morne, et blafarde" (v. 32). In this sad light he is now victimized, both visually and aurally:

> Mon oeil tout effrayé regarde
> Voltiger mille oyseaux de Nuit:
> Les Chauvesouris, les Fresayes
> Dont les cris sont autant de playes
> A l'oreille qui les entend.
>
> (Vv. 33–37)

His expanded reaction is complex, for it echoes the hallucination passage, as well as the relative objectivity of the opening:

> Decoupans l'Air humide et sombre,
> Percent jusqu'où mon corps s'estend,
> Et le muguettent comme une ombre.
>
> (Vv. 38–40)

To amplify the image of physical and emotional pain caused by an assault on his senses, the speaker reintroduces the notion of unwanted and coerced intimacy. At this point, however, he seems to undergo a defensive shift of attitude, a dissociation of consciousness from his beleaguered senses, emotions, and imagination. Thus it is that he describes his reactions with detachment and distance.

Again, without temporal or causal linkage, the speaker passes to the affective narration of another assault, followed by an account of its impact on his emotions and speech:

> Un essaim de maudits Cousins,
> Bruyant d'une fureur extresme,
> Me fait renasquer en moy-mesme
> Contre la saison des raisins.
>
> (Vv. 41–44)

The pattern is repeated when the gnats close in on him:

> L'un sur ma main donne en Sang-süe;
> L'autre sur ma trongne se ruë,
> Me rendant presque tout méseau.

(Vv. 45–47)

The term *méseau* complicates the speaker's reaction. Is he hallucinating again: does he perceive the bites as true leprous lesions? Or does he exploit the ironic detachment of verse 39 by parodying his tendency to magnify pain by analogy? The manner in which he relates his physical reaction suggests the former:

> Je les poursuy, je les attrappe,
> Et sans m'épargner le museau
> Pour les y tuër je me frappe.

(Vv. 48–50)

The lack of a coordinating conjunction in line 48 reinforces the impression of a frenetic mood, but the change to periodic structure in the next two verses implies that the speaker's consciousness has again distanced itself from body and emotion and can thus describe acts and sufferings with maximum detachment. Both qualities are confirmed by the term *museau,* which suggests that on the physical level, at least, he perceives himself as dehumanized, reduced to the same level as his bestial assailants.

Now occurs the last instance of simultaneous composition in the poem's middle passage. Again, without temporal-causal transition, the speaker notices the rats fighting under a table (vv. 53–54): "Où jamais repas délectable / N'apparut aux yeux affamez." He then goes on to relate their acts and intentions— objectively but not without an undertone of bitterness and terror.

At this point—and still without preparation other than the speaker's agony—the second delusion begins. As he recounts a train of distorted images that apparently begins in percepts, the speaker maintains the dissociation of his reasoning consciousness from body, imagination, and feeling. Though he half sees, half imagines "une trouppe de Farfadets" (v. 61), his detached consciousness permits him to turn whimsically analytical, comparing their peculiarities of appearance, "differens de taille, et de forme" (v. 62), and disvaluing individual hobgoblins for quite different reasons, "l'un ridicule, et l'autre énorme" (v. 63), even establishing a mock-heroic analogy: the *trouppe* "s'y deméne en Diables-Cadets" (v. 64). He then states what has long been obvious—

> Ma viziere en est fascinée,
> Mon oüye en est subornée,
> Ma cervelle en est hors de soy.
>
> (Vv. 65–67)

—without, however, acknowledging the lucid consciousness that made the preceding remarks possible. The resumptive verses 68–70 reinforce the paradox of combining a deluded sensorium and a tortured imagination with acuteness of reasoning:

> Bref, ces fabriqueurs d'impostures
> Estalent tout autour de moy
> Leurs grimaces, et leurs postures.

The struggle between defensive consciousness and its coalition of enemies, both internal and external, now reaches its climax. Though betrayed by his "regars en vain sillez" (v. 84) and a "trop credule fantaisie" (v. 85)—which is so possessed and self-terrified that it may collapse—the speaker is fortified by perspicacity. Thus he continues to resist the *cent chimeres hideuses* that present themselves to him: "Je me figure en cette erreur / Qu'on donne le moine à mon ame" (vv. 89–90). Accordingly, he withdraws completely into sleep (vv. 91–92). Thereupon some new and unidentified assailant penetrates him (as always without warning), only to be imagined as an incubus (v. 93), a creature incorporating the worst qualities of all his past assailants: monstrosity, aggressiveness, and voracious sexuality.

Verses 94 and 95 are crucial, marking the formal and psychological transition to the poem's finale: "Et resvant je m'entr'oy gémir. / En fin mes propres cris m'éveillent." The speaker's consciousness is at first far removed from his body and its emotions, hearing groans of pain only faintly, and while dreaming. Consciousness is then forced by the outcries to renounce withdrawal, and so it is that the speaker now reunites, however reluctantly, with emotions and perceptions, reasoning in the dissociated mode of verses 1–40:

> En fin ces Demons s'émerveillent
> D'estre quasi surpris du jour;
> Ils font gille à son arrivée.
>
> (Vv. 96–98)

The final section of the poem consists only of the last two verses—an incomplete instance of simultaneous composition, which reconfirms in a matter-of-fact way (though not without a sense of relief) the reintegration of mental faculties and of mind with body: "Et la diane du tambour / M'avertit que l'Aube est levée" (vv. 99–100). No amplified reaction need be depicted here; it is so strongly implied that explicitness would risk an anticlimactic redundancy.

Formally, then, *Le Mauvais Logement* presents a paradox. The disposition of its elements *seems* rigorous, thanks to the double ternary structure. The poem opens and closes with an objective, stable anecdotal motif in which the speaker's reactions are either included and subordinated or amplified in a separate subsection. The middle, which depicts instability, begins and ends with protracted hallucinations framing a return to the alternance of anecdote and reaction. Despite such tight symmetry, the narrative pattern is not consecutively unified. This is particularly the case in the middle, where the passage from one horror to another is not governed by causality or by time. Events seem to occur at random. Lack of integration on the level of incident is more than offset, however, by the speaker's unusual reasoning, which draws the disparate narrative details into a pattern unity of vastly ironic proportions.

THE CONTRAPASSO

Below the level of consciousness the speaker reasons analogically, conceiving of his nocturnal experience as a reflex or simulacrum of actions that he takes part in or observes by day.

The aggressor in the monologue is the setting itself. Though singular and finite, the inn is perceived as quartering subhuman and supernatural beings without limit: not only the vermin, the nightbirds, the gnats, and the rats, but the hobgoblins and the incubus, as well as malevolent furniture and outfittings. For the speaker nothing less than an epitome of the nonhuman world assaults his body and mind.

Still subliminally, he conceives the plan of attack as military, calling for two strikes. The first, designed to weaken his defenses, consists of exerting irresistible pressure from every direction. Laterally, the tactic is to bind or enclose for restriction of movement: hence the bed is termed a "grabat" (v. 1)—implying a procrustean brevity—and the cover is described as "vilaine" (v. 15)—which among other things suggests tightness. Moreover, the speaker states that the hobgoblins' antics leave his sight "fascinée" (v. 65), that is, bewitched or, more to the point, *bound*. Vertically, the procedure is to keep the victim defenseless and, if possible, humiliated. The speaker describes himself as laid out passively during most of the episode, and (given the full seventeenth-century sense of the term *infame*) he is debased by the "lit de plume" (v. 2). In such a state the victim is prepared for the second and most aggressive phase of the campaign: intimate contact with the ultimate goal of possession. It is this that explains the speaker's emphasis on imagery of penetration and consumption, to say nothing of the sexual overtones contained in the blanket's (and later, the nightbirds') assaults.

Two images sum up the speaker's situation with utmost vividness: the first appears in his analogy, "Et comme un Oyson à la broche, / Je me tourne de tous costez" (vv. 13–14). Locked into place and penetrated, he feels condemned to engage in movement that is not only repetitive but, above all, self-destructive, for it hastens his arrival at the state desired, he thinks, by those who seek to possess and absorb him. The second image occurs in the final stanza, where he is attacked by an incubus—that is, he depicts himself as immobilized, humiliated, and possessed for the satisfaction of his aggressor's selfish purposes.

Now faced with these attacks, the speaker can mount no effective defense, nor can he counterattack. On the somatic level, he even sinks into brutish, inarticulate rage (v. 43). A futile attempt to retaliate leads, as pointed out above, to a sense of dehumanization (vv. 48–50). Finally, he complains that his physical and mental soldiery are one by one stifled, subverted, neutralized, captured or dispersed in panic. After the hobgoblins have bound his *viziere,* for example, his "oüye en est subornée (v. 66). Nor, finally, can his eyes shield him from sights too horrible to endure (vv. 79–80). His imagination is "saisie" (v. 86); his brain, "hors de soy" (v. 67).

Though ostensibly doomed, the speaker survives. Unconsciously, he relates this miracle to two key categories: space and quantity. In both he sees himself and his adversaries as polar opposites. The assailants are multiple, whereas he is single; yet if the dimensions of the inn (which aids and abets the attack) are restricted, and if his limbs, senses, and faculties yield to outside bedevilment, his lucid consciousness, reduced to a minimum, becomes suddenly calm, while entertaining thoughts of sleep (vv. 91–92). Having accepted temporary loss of almost all his physical (and most of his nonstrategic mental) terrain, he sees this minimal consciousness retreat to a point virtually inaccessible to pressure or penetration. There, while awaiting future developments, it appears to suffer nothing but a slight jolt when the body and imagination are rent by their final assailant.

With the submerged, metaphorical view of the attack now in focus, certain symbols become transparent. First, the maneuvers take place: "Au clair de la Lune qui luit / D'une lueur morne, et blafarde" (vv. 31–32). The moon's presence correlates with many of the substances and qualities, as well as passions and states, that the speaker emphasizes during his account. Traditionally linked with the supernatural, the moon is here associated with the weirdly lengthened night, the presence of hobgoblins, and the appearance of an incubus. Moreover, the speaker's passivity, his coerced femininity, and the affliction of his fancy all have a strong lunar resonance. Second, the speaker reports that throughout the *nox irae* "je conte tous les coups de Cloche" (v. 12): in the speaker's mind the mechanically produced sound not only emphasizes the night's endlessness but also sums up the assault of the nonhuman world upon his body and mind.

As the incubus attacks, the whole company of assailants is dispersed by the brilliant light of dawn entering the windows. By this the speaker suggests more than the end of his discomfort and the resumption of waking activities. Indeed, he foreshadows a complete reversal of relations between himself and—in the broadest possible sense—his tormentors. Clearly identified with an army waging war, the speaker almost certainly is implicated in broader skirmishes, incursions, battles for control of key positions, and dispersals of enemy troops. In this context his nocturnal sufferings—the peripheral attacks, the bites, the noise, and the other forms of penetration, plus the struggle to retain control of senses and faculties, and finally the retreat of consciousness—appear as a reversed and scaled-down image of the operations with which he is associated by day. The state of affairs may be summed up through a pair of figurative substitutions: by day the entire contained entity (the army) aggressively seeks to take possession of the entire container (the territory where the inn is located); by night, however, part of the container (the inn) afflicts in like manner a part of the contained entity (the speaker).

This implicit symmetry is reinforced by a second pair of symbols. Whereas the nocturnal engagement takes place under the sign of Diana and to the accompaniment of the bell, the day's operations are announced by the "diane du tambour" (v. 99) which sounds as "l'Aube est levée" (v. 100). In contrast with the dreary bell, the drum commands the hearer to rise and prepare for action, to assist directly or indirectly in the conquest or occupation of the territory that only moments before was seeking to control and vanquish him. Similarly, the sun, which traditionally represents masculinity, rationality, and a propensity for action, is an emblem for whoever answers the summons of the drum.

The speaker's sense of a parallel between the explicit night and the implicit day gains its full meaning in his casual remarks about the setting itself. There, he states:

> Je passe les plus tristes heures
> Qui dans les mortelles Demeures
> Puissent affliger les Esprits.
>
> (Vv. 5–7)

The stress on *mortelles* intimates that from his viewpoint the only place worse than the inn is the locale where souls suffer *im*mortally. The gosling simile (vv. 12–13) portrays the speaker's forced suspension over fire; the natural and supernatural fauna of the inn have unmistakable traits: the gnats are "maudits" (v. 41), the *farfadets* are like "Diables-Cadets" (v. 64) and disport themselves in "infernales nigeries" (v. 73). All, finally, are "Demons" (v. 96). The setting, in other words, is a temporary and earthly hell, where the speaker suffers, in the image of his crimes, or those of the army he accompanies.

Through the submerged image of the *contrapasso*, then, the disparate elements of the frenetic, fragmented narrative are resolved into a unified whole.

Nonconsecutive unity occurs in many disrupted temporal lyrics of early seventeenth-century France. To Saint-Amant's nature poems,[14] Malherbe's last revisions of *Les Larmes de Saint-Pierre,* and Théophile de Viau's epistle to Louis XIII on his exile may be added (among others) Maynard's *Ode* ("L'Astre du jour a beau sortir de l'onde"), the "Songe" of Sigogne, and Tristan L'Hermite's "Extase d'un baiser."

1. Smith, pp. 117–31.

2. Elder Olson, *The Poetry of Dylan Thomas,* pp. 42–52; idem, "The Lyric," p. 218.

3. All quotations from the sonnets are from Pierre de Ronsard, *Les Amours,* ed. Henri Weber and Catherine Weber. The text of *Amours diverses,* 17, appears on pp. 461–62.

4. *Amours,* pp. 431–32.

5. Ibid., pp. 385–86.

6. Pierre de Ronsard, *Oeuvres complètes,* Laumonier 2:214–16.

7. *Amours,* pp. 55–56.

8. Cf. Smith, pp. 127–28. I would contend that simultaneous composition may take any tense, not merely the present, as Smith argues, since an ongoing action (and the immediate reaction it provokes) may be remembered or anticipated.

9. *Amours,* p. 394.

10. Ibid., p. 40.

11. Ibid., p. 59.

12. For an excellent treatment of discontinuity in certain works of Ronsard, see Terence C. Cave, *The Cornucopian Text,* pp. 223–71.

13. All quotations from the caprice refer to Saint-Amant, *Oeuvres,* ed. Jean Lagny, 2:144–49.

14. For a full treatment of simultaneous composition in Saint-Amant's nature poetry, see Robert T. Corum, Jr., *Other Worlds and Other Seas.*

3

Théophile de Viau
Le Matin

The least common form of serial lyricism originates in a noncausal, nonlogical matrix. Altogether typical is the popular song *Les douze mois de l'année,* which follows the order of the occidental calendar. Rimbaud's sonnet *Les Voyelles* is equally representative, though in a more complex manner. While using Roman letters for the sake of clarity, the poet develops his theme by following the order of the Greek alphabet. In both cases poetic succession does not reflect a natural or "scientific" pattern, but one that has been established and maintained by the force of tradition alone.[1]

In late sixteenth- and early seventeenth-century France the conventional structure most widely used in the lyric was derived from the religious meditation.[2] A rapid survey of its treatment—with emphasis on a typical poet's solution to the problem of fragmentation and rupture—will provide useful background to discussion of Théophile de Viau's *Le Matin.*

Modeled on the ancient process popularized by Saint Ignatius Loyola in his *Vrays exercices spirituels,* the activity is tripartite. The meditant begins (after an elective preliminary prayer) by drawing on memory and imagination to "compose" the scene that he will contemplate; he then reasons on its significance; finally, he addresses an appropriate object of religious sentiment. In La Ceppède's *théorème,* "Dez qu'on eut achevé cet injuste supplice" (III, 32), for example, the speaker first narrates the Passion of Christ and the just execution of the two thieves, whose very presence augments Christ's humiliation by the Jews; the speaker then realizes that the incident is necessary as a fulfillment of prophecy and as the climax to a collective career of imposture; finally, he directly addresses Christ, expressing grief and indignation at the unparalleled affront.[3]

Irregularities abound in the *Théorèmes,* but close analysis reveals that the poet has usually embroidered on tradition, not rent it asunder. For instance, the many individual sonnets containing only one of the three required elements almost always prove to be predictable sections of long sequences that *do* adhere to the ternary pattern. The well-known text "L'Autel des vieux parfums" (III, 23), which lacks both composition and prayer, appears in the analytical movement of a complete meditation on the cross (III, 10–31). More problematic is the sonnet that exhibits two or three constituents unconventionally linked. In "Achevant ces propos, d'un long baiser jumeau" (III, 13), the composition is interrupted by prayer. It is necessary, however, to distinguish between fundamental, contributory, and derivative structures. In the seemingly disrupted sonnet, composition is—and remains—essential; the prayer is merely parenthetical, serving to heighten the scene's emotional intensity.

It happens, of course, that a certain number of La Ceppède's *théorèmes* simply fail, in the sense that they do not achieve or contribute to consecutive unity and are not salvaged by any compensatory device. Characteristically, these are "free-floating" analyses, like "Jesus donc ne veut point ce baiser refuser" (I, 47), which follows no composition and leads to no prayer.

La Ceppède was clearly a transitional poet. By allowing some analyses to float freely, he based his practice on that of his immediate predecessors, who merely let their fragmentary or ruptured sequences stand *telles quelles.* But his tendency to appropriate other irregular structures by devices of hierarchy and subordination aligns him at least in part with the subjects of this essay. Nevertheless, La Ceppède did not arrange the bits and pieces of ruptured sequences into nonconsecutive patterns, nor did he use compensatory devices. Thus it is possible to distinguish his art from that of Malherbe, Saint-Amant, and above all

Théophile de Viau, who, in *Le Matin,* shattered and restructured a form as conventional as the meditation itself.

Le Matin

L'Aurore sur le front du jour
Seme l'azur, l'or et l'yvoire;
Et le Soleil, lassé de boire,
Commence son oblique tour.

5   Les chevaux au sortir de l'onde,
De flamme et de clarté couverts,
La bouche et les naseaux ouverts,
Ronflent la lumière du monde.

La Lune fuit devant nos yeux;
10   La nuict a retiré ses voiles;
Peu à peu le front des estoilles
S'unit à la couleur des Cieux.

Desjà la diligente Avette
Boit la marjolaine et le tin,
15   Et revient riche du butin
Qu'elle a prins sur le mont Hymette.

Je voy le genereux Lion,
Qui sort de sa demeure creuse,
Herissant sa perruque affreuse,
20   Qui faict fuyr Endimion.

Sa Dame entrant dans les boccages
Compte les Sangliers qu'elle a pris,
Ou devale chez les esprits
Errant aux sombres marescages.

25   Je voy les Agneaux bondissans
Sur les bleds qui ne font que naistre:
Cloris chantant les mene paistre,
Parmy ces costeaux verdissans.

Les oyseaux d'un joyeux ramage
30   En chantant semblent adorer
La lumiere qui vient dorer
Leur cabinet et leur plumage.

La charruë escorche la plaine;
Le bouvier qui suit les seillons
35   Presse de voix et d'aiguillons
Le couple de boeufs qui l'entraîne.

Alix appreste son fuseau;
Sa mere qui luy faict la tasche,
Presse le chanvre qu'elle attache
40   A sa quenoüille de roseau.

Une confuse violence
Trouble le calme de la nuict,
Et la lumiere avec le bruit
Dissipent l'ombre et le silence.

45   Alidor cherche à son resveil
L'ombre d'Iris qu'il a baisée,
Et pleure en son ame abusée
La fuitte d'un si doux sommeil.

Les bestes sont dans leur taniere,
50   Qui tremblent de voir le Soleil;
L'homme remis par le sommeil
Reprend son oeuvre coustumiere.

Le forgeron est au fourneau,
Oy comme le charbon s'alume;
55   Le fer rouge dessus l'enclume
Etincelle sous le marteau.

Ceste chandelle semble morte:
Le jour la faict esvanouyr;
Le Soleil vient nous esblouyr:
60   Voy qu'il passe au travers la porte.

Il est jour: levons-nous Philis,
Allons à nostre jardinage
Voir s'il est comme ton visage,
Semé de roses et de lis.[4]

ALBA LONGA

The principle governing linear development in *Le Matin* originates in the custom of illicit lovers, who—singly or together—rise at dawn and separate. The same practice serves as the basis of the *alba*. It would be difficult, however, to prove that Théophile knew any medieval examples of the genre. On the other hand, like the *trouvères* who created the vernacular *alba*, Théophile must have known an important classical model, Ovid's *Amores* 1. 13.[5] (In addition to the dawn/departure formula, several other of that elegy's structural peculiarities also occur in *Le Matin*, namely, the reference to Endymion,[6] and the

account of occupations normally pursued after sunrise, especially tilling,[7] and spinning.[8])

Obviously, however, *Le Matin* radically deviates from the
convention: though the lovers *may* depart from their trysting
place, they will not separate. Instead, if the speaker has his way,
they will pursue a new activity—in unison. Were this deviation
insufficient in itself to preclude consecutive unity, another formal problem—the length, complexity, and disjointedness of the
speaker's opening description—certainly would do so.

The Sunne Rising (verses 1–56)

The poem opens on a note of extreme ambiguity. It is
not clear who the speaker is or where, whether he is perceiving,
imagining, remembering, reasoning, or engaging in a combination of these activities, whether his monologue is interior or
dramatic—and if dramatic, whom he addresses. It is only in the
second section that most of these problems are resolved.

The speaker begins by describing the dawn in the manner of
countless poets (including Ovid):[9] Aurora appears and flings
colored light; while the moon flees and the stars fade, the sun, a
golden chariot drawn by fire-breathing horses, arises from the
sea to begin its customary circuit.[10] There follows an account of
dawn's effect—the resumption of diurnal occupations—but passage from one item to the next is not rigorously determinate.
Instead, the speaker presents a series of loosely associated
tableaux, opening with celestial and closing with earthly activities or passivities. This implies that the verb "voir" (v. 17) refers
less to perception than to an alloy of memory and imagination.

Pictured first is the bee (vv. 13–16), linked to the preceding
section by images of drinking, movement, and union. Both the
sun and the bee have imbibed—though on radically different
scales (vv. 3 and 14); the sun's horses and the bee are, respec-
tively, ascending and descending (vv. 5 and 15–16); finally, just
as "le front des estoilles / S'unit à la couleur des Cieux" (vv.
11–12), so the *marjolain* and the *tin* are combined in the bee's
crop. (The reference to Mount Hymettus is of philological interest, for it is from this peak that Ovid's Aurora dispels darkness
from the world.)

The suggestive link between the bee and the lion (vv. 17–20) is
negative. The two creatures are, for example, opposites in size

and power. Moreover, the bee returns to an enclosure—the hive—whereas the lion emerges from one—his "demeure creuse" (v. 18). Finally, the bee is active but the lion has yet to begin his daily depredations. (When he asserts that bristling his mane, the lion makes Endymion flee [vv. 19–20], the speaker confuses the hypothetical with the real for the sake of creating a brilliant hyperbole. The speaker means, of course, that the lion's *perruque* is so frightful that it *would* awaken the eternal sleeper and frighten him away if only Endymion were susceptible.)

The ambiguous possessive adjective *sa* in verse 21 leaves some doubt about the identity of the Dame. Does the speaker refer to the lioness (an equally predatory member of the pride), or to Selene-Diana, goddess of the moon, a huntress who loved Endymion and visited him in his *demeure creuse*? That the subject of this stanza goes to visit marsh sprites (vv. 23–24) tilts the interpretation in Diana's favor, for she was attended by a band of water nymphs. In either case, the transition from the preceding stanza is effected by the contrast between "entrant" (v. 21) and "sort" (v. 18), along with its synonym, in this context, "fuyr" (v. 20).

The bounding lambs following a shepherdess (vv. 25–28) stand in antithesis with the lion and "esprits / Errant" (vv. 23–24), just as their respective settings contrast with one another: "sombres marescages" (v. 24) and "bleds . . . costeaux verdissans" (vv. 26–28).

The description of birds warbling at the light that decorates their retreat (vv. 29–32) articulates with the preceding tableau by the repetition of the key word "chantant" (vv. 27 and 30) and the related "ramage" (v. 29).

The tiller's stanza (vv. 33–36) conjoins with that of the birds by negative suggestion: undisturbed "plumage" (v. 32) contrasts sharply with the surface of the soil, which his plow "escorche" (v. 33); and the birds' sequestered "cabinet" (v. 32) stands in opposition to the open "plaine" (v. 33) on which he labors. The total effect is one of antithesis between a closed, tranquil environment decorated by animal life and an open, violent setting dominated by man.

From the image of oxen, driven by the tiller, to that of Alix preparing to spin (vv. 37–40), there is a great distance, bridged associatively by the formal similarity between "aiguillons" (v.

35) and the "fuseau" (v. 37), as well as the repetition of the term *presse*—with its play on its literal and figurative meanings (vv. 35 and 39).

The following tableau presents an unusual problem:

> Une confuse violence
> Trouble le calme de la nuict,
> Et la lumiere avec le bruit
> Dissipent l'ombre et le silence.

(Vv. 41–44)

These lines serve to recall that the activities described before and after them are occurring simultaneously at the break of day, i.e., that the time required for reading or recitation of so many vignettes does not entail the forward movement of the poem's pseudonarrative time by so much as a second. The *strophe-rappel* is linked to those of the spinner and tiller by the antithesis between orderly work performed in the latter, over against the "confuse violence" (v. 41) of dawn.

Linking the *strophe-rappel* to the conventional alba ending are the repetition of the word "ombre" (vv. 44 and 46), the analogy between Iris's disappearance and the dispersal of night, and the abrupt transitions from night to dawn (vv. 43–44) and from sleeping to waking (v. 45), plus the depiction of an aggrieved lover separating, or separated, from his beloved at dawn (vv. 45–48). Why *Le Matin* does not terminate at this point is obvious. Developmentally this stanza lacks closural force, as it leaves the speaker's identity and situation—as well as the nature and purpose of his acts—in a state of unresolved ambiguity. To stop at this point would leave the poem formally incomplete and thus disunified. Moreover, no special terminal features—allusive or stylistic—are present to help arrest expectation of further development and to prepare for the end of the discourse.

The opening section's penultimate stanza (vv. 49–52)—which describes small animals trembling in their burrows and men going to their accustomed work—articulates with the Alidor tableau on two levels: that of analogy (between Iris's flight and the concealment of the prospective prey) and that of imagery (for interiority is denoted by the synonyms "en" [v. 47] and "dans" [v. 49]. Finally, the smith's labor and perception prolong the idea of "oeuvre" (v. 52).

The Closed Compass (verses 57–64)

Having set the scene at extraordinary length, the speaker finally prepares to take action or exhort to it, stressing the paradox of darkness at dawn and the chiaroscuro resulting from light's penetration of the door (vv. 57–60). The visual and aural associations of "étincelle" (v. 56) facilitate the transition from the preceding stanza.

There follows an invitation from the speaker to Philis: not to separate but to join him in the garden where they can test his analogy between the coloring of her face and that of the flowers. The repetition of the verb *voir* (vv. 60 and 63) and the repeated image of passing through a portal (vv. 60 and 62) smooth the transition from scene to act.

The last stanzas constitute a model finale. First and most obviously, they complete the convention, though in an unexpected and perverse way. They also resolve the poem's ambiguities by revealing the speaker's identity, situation, and action: he is a lover who greets his waking mistress with a dramatic monologue rich in recollections and fancies focused on the time of day, as well as the actions and sufferings of other creatures—all of this as a prelude to departure for a "task" that awaits them outside their dwelling. Because the finale is unexpected and potentially disconcerting, it is necessary that closure be as strong as possible. And it is, thanks to the poet's use of special terminal features. The poem concludes with a *pointe* whose open/shut structure arrests expectation of further development:

> Allons à nostre jardinage
> Voir s'il est comme ton visage,
> Semé de roses et de lis.

> (Vv. 62–64)

Beginning with verse 54, there is also a major shift in syntax— away from the simple declarative patterns that dominate the poem to a series of imperatives ("oy" [v. 54], "Voy" [v. 60], "Allons" [v. 62]), the last of which seems to suggest a conclusion drawn from the preceding materials. Moreover, the vocabulary of the final verses recapitulates—explicitly, by synonymy, or by metaphor—many of the terms found in the opening stanzas, e.g., "front" (v. 1) / "visage" (v. 63), *semer* (vv. 2

and 64), and "yvoire (v. 2) / "lis" (v. 64). This device provides a conclusive sense of "having come full circle."

Thus the poem opens, unfolds, and ends, its sequential unity blasted by a long, loosely articulated digression. Closer examination of the imagery and symbolism, however, points to the pervasive analogical reasoning, which not only redeems but metaphysically necessitates the dislocated exposition.

A PHAËTON OF THE MIND

As indicated above, a portion of *Le Matin* originates in Ovid's *Metamorphoses* 2, whereas generally the poem's structure has marked affinities with that of the thirteenth elegy of the same poet's *Amores* 1. These would be little more than marginally interesting historical facts if they did not bear directly on the solution to the poem's formal problems.

In the section of the *Metamorphoses* from which the two early lines are adapted, the narrator recounts the catastrophic ride taken by Phaëton in his father Apollo's sun chariot. Careening back and forth between heaven and earth, Phaëton saw many objects: great cities set aflame by the car, the Alps, the Moon, and—of greatest interest here—the constellations. These he perceives not as groups of stars but as the figures whose cardinal points the stars traditionally indicate:

> For the first time the cold bears grew hot with the rays of the sun and tried, though all in vain, to plunge into the sea. And the Serpent, which lies nearest the icy pole, ever before harmless because sluggish with the cold, now grew hot and conceived great frenzy from that fire. They say that you also, Boötes, fled in terror, slow though you were, and held back by your clumsy ox-cart. (Vv. 171–77)

Note that at least one of these, Boötes, is engaged in his *oeuvre coustumiere*. This theme of labor at (or soon after) dawn is a concern of the speaker in Ovid's elegy as well: he hates sunrise in part at least because it announces the resumption of toil:

> You cheat boys of their slumber and give them over to the master, that their tender hands may yield to the cruel stroke; and likewise many do you send as sponsors before the court, to undergo great losses at a single word. You bring joy neither to lawyer nor to pleader; each is ever compelled to rise for cases anew. (Vv. 17–22)

Now close examination of the text strongly suggests that in the central descriptive stanzas the speaker fuses and transforms the two Ovidian motifs: that of earthly loss and labor at dawn, and that of the living constellations.

The bee, already associated with celestial activities by its operations on Mount Hymettus, parallels the constellation Apes (renamed Mosca), found to the east of Aries. The lion, distinguished by its terrifying *perruque,* is analogous to the fierce Leo Major, two of whose brightest stars, sigma and upsilon, are found in the mane. There being no lioness in the skies, it is even more certain that the *Dame* of verse 21 is Endymion's lady, the moon goddess Selene-Diana. Her descent into darkness is an analogue for the moon's setting. The *agneaux* represent Aries, which have been perceived as a flock of sheep. Meanwhile, the *oyseaux* are analogues to the Pleiades (also known as the Colombae). The tiller goading his oxen to pull the plow is burlesque analogue of Apollo himself, goading his horses to pull the sun chariot. The filial Alix—whose name suggests nobility or honesty—typifies the Lost Pleiade or Virgo. The latter holds a palm, symbol of rebirth, not a distaff, although the distaff might symbolize renewal for, by its action, the hemp will change its mode of existence, its potentialities, and its ends. The lovers, Alidor and Iris, symbolize Orion and his mistress Eos (Aurora by a different name), who naturally disappears moments before the break of day. The *bestes* in their burrows are analogous with Lepus, seen in the sky crouching low on the horizon, almost trampled by Orion. And finally, the *forgeron*—who seems remarkably like Vulcan—resembles the sun itself, for which Vulcan was sometimes taken as a symbol. The identifications converge and form one term of a master analogy crucial to the speaker's thought and hence to the unity of *Le Matin.* As an earthbound, diurnal equivalent to a round-the-clock labor force in heaven, they constitute a microcosm. Significantly, however, the speaker excludes his mistress and himself from this universal scheme of labor and loss. They correspond to no constellation, they do not labor—physically, at least—and they do not separate, as social conventions dictate.

The lovers' anomalous standing receives further emphasis in images repeated by the speaker throughout the poem. There are at least three great networks that implicate the celestial and terrestrial domains, as well as the lovers'. These are movement, substance, and sound.

The imagery of movement includes three subtypes, which in one case overlap: the vertical, the oblique, and the emergent. Just as the sun's horses "sort[ent] de l'onde" (v. 5), the lion "sort de sa demeure creuse" (v. 18)—both to begin their daily tasks. By contrast, the lovers will emerge from their shelter, but not to engage in physical labor; instead they will visit their garden, and test the speaker's analogy. The sun emerges from the sea and rises, just as the bee flies up to Mount Hymettus, and the growing lambs, full of surplus vitality, leap up on the verdure—as part of their daily routine. But if and when Philis arises in response to her lover's request (v. 61), her sole purpose will be to test poetic comparisons. Meanwhile light falls from above, the bee comes back down from Mount Hymettus, and Diane *dévale* among her attendant sprites, just as the plow cuts deeply into the soil, rabbits burrow, and the smith strikes the anvil. In none of this downward movement, however, do the lovers participate. Perhaps a "minus factor," this phenomenon points yet again to the lovers' freedom from ordinary labor; it may also imply their exemption from humble and humbling acts or preoccupations. Finally there is curved or slanting movement: the sun will make an "oblique tour" (v. 4), and Alix will spin a wheel. The lover, too, makes an *oblique tour,* but in a sense wholly different from that of verse 4—he will think and speak in equivocal, indirect, and analogically rich terms—a fact by which he points (obliquely!) to his unusual rank.

The imagery of substance and sound give further clues. The universe of loss and labor—macrocosm and microcosm—are directly cognizable in terms of conventional categories—animal, vegetable, and mineral; fire, air, earth, and water. But his mistress's face is ineffable in ordinary language; it can be apprehended only by an analogy, ingeniously provided by her lover. In the universe at large, moreover, sound is generally noise or simple patterns of tone: the snorting of Apollo's horses, Cloris's song, the warbling of birds, the tiller's shouts, Alidor's weeping, and so on. The lover, however, whose speech the poem itself more than amply illustrates, is, as already indicated, the master of the *oblique tour*: equivocal, dovetailing, implication-laden discourse—in short, *poetry.*

NY HOMME NY HIMAGE

To sum up, all the personages in *Le Matin* are wholly subject to most ordinary rules—except the lovers. All—except the lovers—are not more than minor terms in a universal analogy of loss and labor. The lovers' various characteristics and action distinguish them as marginal participants ultimately transcending this scheme. Like mankind they are earthbound and physically limited. Like lesser divinities they are superior in power and dignity to mankind. But above all, they together resemble the supreme divinity: the mistress, like God, is not directly knowable and is declared capable of self-reflexive thought (no other personage in the poem can make that claim); but her thinking is restricted to the figurative terms provided by her privileged intimate, the speaker, a man endowed with the power to create verbal equivalents to the divinely ordained analogies of which the universe is constituted. In short, the lover portrays his mistress and himself as constituting a set apart, intersecting those of man, the gods, and God. Exceptions to nearly all hierarchies, they are comparable to the lovers described by Donne, who are a microuniverse and a law unto themselves.

The fragments of the conventional sequence are thus resolved into a lavish description of a state or condition of being, presented contrastively, aspect by aspect. In terms of this descriptive unity, the violation of the literary rule, itself a mere reflection of a broken social rule, is not merely appropriate but absolutely indispensable to the coherence of the poem.

Outside the devotional sequences, lyrics with "conventional" structures are relatively rare during *le premier dix-septième siècle*. Any account of those which deviate from pre-established norms but attain nonconsecutive unity nevertheless would certainly include two very well-known texts: Malherbe's *Consolation à M. du Périer* in its last revision and Saint-Amant's *sonnet à treize vers*.

1. See Smith, pp. 109–17.

2. For much of the data from which I draw the inferences to follow, I am indebted to Terence C. Cave's indispensable study *Devotional Poetry in France ca. 1570–1613* and Nancy Hafer's "The Art of Metaphor in La Ceppède's *Théorèmes* of 1613," as well as her important refinement of Cave's

theory,"Developmental Patterns in La Ceppède's *Théorèmes*." All of these studies stem, of course, from Louis L. Martz's classic, *The Poetry of Meditation*. Regrettably, Paul Chilton's cogent anticonventionalist argument in *The Poetry of Jean de La Ceppède* (Oxford: Oxford University Press, 1977) was unavailable to me as I completed this essay.

3. All citations of La Ceppède refer to *Les Théorèmes sur le sacré mystère de nostre rédemption*.

4. All citations of "Le Matin" refer to Théophile de Viau, *Oeuvres poétiques*, 1:13–16. I have normalized the punctuation.

5. See Rudolph Schevill in *Ovid and the Renaissance in Spain*, p.126.

6. Ovid, vv. 43–44, cf. Théophile, v. 20. All references to the *Amores* are to Ovid, *Heroides and Amores*, in the Loeb Classical Library text and translation of Grant Showerman, pp. 369–73.

7. V. 15 of Ovid, cf. vv. 33–36 of Théophile.

8. Vv. 23–24 of Ovid, cf. vv. 37–40 of Théophile.

9. Cf. Ovid's *Metamorphoses* 7. 702–4. The colors flung by Aurora resemble those of the sun's palace in *Metamorphoses* 2. 2–4. All references are to the Loeb Classical Library text and translation of Frank Justus Miller, vol. 1.

10. Cf. Ovid's *Metamorphoses* 2. 84–85, 154–55, already noted by Streicher in Viau, *Oeuvres poétiques*, p. 13.

PART TWO
BEYOND INDETERMINACY

4

François de Maynard
Ode ("Alcipe, reviens dans nos Bois")

When the linkage of lyric elements obeys the principle of suggestion—that is, when it follows the promptings of the speaker's thought alone, rather than external custom, the laws of cause and effect, or the canons of logic—the result is an associative structure.[1] Suggestion of course is bipolar: it may be positive or negative. Just as similars and proximates (in time or space) may evoke one another, so too may dissimilars and things widely separated. Even the constituents of serial development are subject to this principle. Any conventional element may, for example, remind the speaker of a related one; cause may recall effect (and vice versa); or a step in a logical process may occasion thought of another step. The order, however, is never necessary: it does not reflect a rigorous procedure. Instead, it is merely probable, mirroring the more or less controlled movements of the speaker's soul.

Unless composed in a self-terminating, fixed prosodic form (the sonnet, for example), the set of associations could continue indefinitely, and even in the fixed form, special terminating devices must be used to assure closure (as opposed to mere stoppage of the speaker's activity). Among these features are allusions to finality, unqualified statements, and radical deviations from the thematic and stylistic norms of the poem as a whole, any of which may be reinforced by puns, parallelism, or antithesis.

Despite its emphasis on a divorce between currents of mind and the "rules" of the external world, the preceding does not imply that associative structure is a modernist or late romantic invention. A glance at the earlier French lyric makes the reason clear. Consider the following lines:

> Onques ne fui sans amor
> N'yver n'esté.
> Tos jors est li solaus chaus
> En plain aoust.
> Il ne me chaut qu'il me coust
> Mes que je l'aie.
> C'est à Saint-Germain en Laie
> Que li rois iert.[2]

Through verse six in the stanza of a thirteenth-century *fatrasie,* associative passage from one statement to another is assured by the obsessive notion of heat, both literal and figurative (*amor, esté, solaus chaus, chaut*). In other words, similars evoke one another. By moving through the rhyme (*l'aie/Laie*) to a theme not obviously related to *chaleur* the last two verses cut the series off and thus effectively close the *strophe.* Clément Marot continued this madcap manner in his *épistres en coq-à-l'âne,* for example:

> Si j'eusse plus tost mys au net
> Ce coq à l'ane, Colinet,
> Ton renom n'en feust abaissé.
> Or aprens bien ton a b c;
> Tu seras maugré mesdisans,
> De l'eaige de huict ou dix ans.[3]

The humoristic tradition culminated, of course, in the notorious *sonnet de Porchères, Sur les yeux de Madame la duchesse de Beaufort,* of which only a few lines need be cited:

> Ce ne sont pas des yeux, ce sont plustost des Dieux:
> Ils ont dessus les rois la puissance absolue.
> Dieux, non, ce sont des Cieux: ils ont la couleur bleue
> Et le mouvement prompt comme celui des Cieux.[4]

Long misread as the ultimate in *mièvrerie,* this sonnet actually burlesques petrarchan clichés by replacing their usual narrative or discursive arrangement with phonetic suggestion (*yeux-Dieux-*

Cieux) and the topos of contradiction. Triteness of idea and sentiment not only subsists, but actually receives greater emphasis because of Porchère's developmental strategy.

If associative progression is not new, neither is it invariably comic, even in its earliest manifestations. In Du Bellay's *Songe ou Vision,* for example, the speaker imagines buildings composed of precious materials, their synthesis attributable to traditional meanings, as filtered through his consciousness.

> Je vy hault eslevé sur columnes d'ivoire,
> Dont les bases estoient du plus riche metal,
> A chapiteaux d'albastre, et frizes de crystal,
> Le double front d'un arc dressé pour la memoire.[5]

Finally, in the "analytical" passages of his *Théorèmes,* Jean de La Ceppède occasionally substitutes associative recall and juxtaposition for logical inquiry. The often anthologized sonnet on white is a typical case:

> Blanc est le vestment du grand Pere sans âge,
> Blancs sont les courtisans de sa maison,
> Blanc est de son esprit l'étincelant pennage,
> Blanche est de son Agneau la brillante Toison.[6]

Maynard's *Ode* "Alcipe, reviens dans nos Bois" belongs to the second tradition[7] of early French associative poetry—that in which the personage seriously strives to persuade himself, an auditor, or the reader of the rightness or wrongness of a concept, feeling, or course of action. The "didactic" unity is more fully realized here than in other poems of the same type, however, largely because of Maynard's ingenious integration of the associative process itself with the indirect elements of proof.

Ode

> Alcipe, reviens dans nos Bois.
> Tu n'as que trop suivy les Rois,
> Et l'infidelle espoir dont tu fais ton Idole:
> Quelque bon-heur qui seconde tes Voeux,
> 5   Ils n'arresteront pas le Temps qui tousjours vole,
> Et qui d'un triste blanc va peindre tes cheveux.
>
> La Cour mesprise ton Encens.
> Ton Rival monte, et tu descens,
> Et dans le Cabinet le Favory te joüe.

10   Que t'a servy de fléchir le genous
Devant un Dieu fragile et fait d'un peu de boüe,
Qui soûfre et qui vieillit pour mourir comme nous?

      Romps tes Fers, bien qu'ils soient dorez.
      Fuy le injustes adorez,
15   Et descens dans toy-mesme à l'exemple du Sage.
      Tu vois de prés ta derniere saison:
Tout le Monde connoist ton nom et ton visage,
Et tu n'és pas connu de ta propre raison.

      Ne forme que des saints desirs,
20   Et te sépare des plaisirs
Dont la molle douceur te fait aymer la vie.
      Il faut quiter le séjour des Mortels,
Il faut quiter Filis, Amarante et Silvie,
A qui ta fole Amour esleve des Autels.

25   Il faut quiter l'Ameublement
      Qui nous cache pompeusement,
Sous de la toile d'or, le plastre de ta Chambre.
      Il faut quiter ces Jardins tousjours vers,
Que l'haleine des Fleurs parfume de son ambre,
30   Et qui font des Printemps au milieu des Hyvers.

      C'est en vain que loin des hazars
      Où courent les Enfans de Mars,
Nous laissons reposer nos mains et nos courages;
      Et c'est en vain que la fureur des eaux,
35   Et l'insolent Borée, Artisan des naufrages,
Font à l'abry du Port retirer nos Vaisseaux.

      Nos avons beau nous mesnager,
      Et beau prévenir le danger,
La Mort n'est pas un mal que le Prudent évite
40   Il n'est raison, adresse, ny conseil
Qui nous puisse exempter d'aller où le Cocite
Arrouse des Païs inconnus au Soleil.

      Le cours de nos ans est borné,
      Et quand nostre heure aura sonné,
45   Cloton ne voudra plus grossir nostre fusée.
      C'est une Loy, non pas un chastiment,
Que la necessité qui nous est imposée
De servir de pasture aux vers du Monument.

      Resous-toi d'aller chez les Mors;
50   Ny la Race, ny les Tresors

Ne sçauroient t'empescher d'en augmenter le nombre.
   Le Potentat le plus grand de nos jours
Ne sera rien qu'un nom, ne sera rien qu'une ombre,
Avant qu'un demy-siecle ait achevé son cours.

55   On n'est guere loin du matin
           Qui doit terminer le Destin
     Des superbes Tyrans du Danube et du Tage.
        Ils font les Dieux dans le Monde Chrestien:
     Mais ils n'auront sur toy que le triste avantage
60   D'infecter un Tombeau plus riche que le tien.

           Et comment pourrions-nous durer?
           Le Temps, qui doit tout devorer,
     Sur le fer et la pierre exerce son empire;
        Il abatra ces fermes Bastimens
65   Qui n'offrent à nos yeux que marbre et que porphire,
     Et qui jusqu'aux Enfers portent leurs fondemens.

           On cherche en vain les belles Tours
           Où Paris cacha ses Amours,
     Et d'où ce Féneant vit tant de funerailles.
70   Rome n'a rien de son antique orgueil,
     Et le vuide enfermé de ses vieilles murailles
     N'est qu'un affreux objet et qu'un vaste cercueil.

           Mais tu dois avecque mespris
           Regarder ces petits débris:
75   Le Temps amenera la fin de toutes choses;
        Et ce beau Ciel, ce lambris azuré,
     Ce Theatre, où l'Aurore espanche tant de Roses,
     Sera bruslé des feux dont il est esclairé.

           Le grand Astre qui l'embellit
80   Fera sa Tombe de son Lit:
     L'Air ne fermera plus ny Gresles, ny Tonnerres;
        Et l'Univers, qui dans son large tour
     Voit courir tant de Mers et fleurir tant de Terres,
     Sans sçavoir où tomber, tombera quelque jour.[8]

L'ESPRIT DE GÉOMÉTRIE

   An argumentative address, the ode *appears* to advance
logically. It opens with an imperative—whose tone is that of an
urgent plea, not a command: "Alcipe, reviens dans nos Bois" (v.
1). The speaker then shifts at once to the presentation of supporting arguments (vv. 2–12, 31–84), interrupted only by an excursus

on the acts required of Alcipe if he is to change not merely the style but above all the substance of his life (vv. 13–30). Closer examination, however, reveals that an arational principle governs the poem's developmental structure.

Vanitas vanitatum (verses 2–12)

There are many questions the speaker might have answered in the section that immediately follows the generating imperative. The choice of *why* over *how* was, if not arbitrary, then at least not prescribed by logical necessity. Rather, he shifts from the urgent appeal to the first set of reasons by negative suggestion, that is, by the opposition of *Bois* (v. 1), a place of refuge favorable to introspection, and *Rois* (v. 2), symbolic of the court, a place of humiliation and futility:

> La Cour mesprise ton Encens.
> Ton Rival monte, et tu descens,
> Et dans le Cabinet le Favory je joüe.
> Que t'a servy de fléchir le genous.
>
> (Vv. 7–10)

The speaker's first arguments exemplify the topos, *vanitas vanitatum*: it matters little that the favor Alcipe has assiduously sought at court was finally denied; happiness, after all, cannot halt time or, consequently, prevent death, to which even the *grands* are subject. This argument, however, is inconclusive. It does not follow that as a mortal and a fallen courtier, Alcipe must retire to *nos Bois*.

"Aequo pulsat pede" (verses 31–84)

In verse 31 the change of subject is associative. After the seductive description of *Jardins tousjours vers*: "Que l'haleine des Fleurs parfume de son ambre, / Et qui font des Printemps au milieu des Hyvers" (vv. 29–30), the obsessive, paired ideas of vanity and death reassert themselves by simple opposition. It is no accident that in the opening stanzas of this section the expressive *c'est en vain* appears twice: "C'est en vain que loin des hazars" (v. 31) and "Et c'est en vain que la fureur des eaux" (v. 34), twice more counting the synonymous expression *avoir beau*: "Nous avons beau nous mesnager, / Et beau prévenir le danger" (vv. 37–38).

The final section opens by announcing at great length the inevitability of death, the perishability of matter, and the immortality of the soul:

> Il n'est raison, adresse, ny conseil
> Qui nous puisse exempter d'aller où le Cocite
> Arrouse des Païs inconnus au Soleil.
>
> Le cours de nos ans est borné,
> Et quand nostre heure aura sonné,
> Cloton ne voudra plus grossir nostre fusée.
> C'est une Loy, non pas un chastiment,
> Que la necessité qui nous est imposeé
> De servir de pasture aux vers du Monument.
>
> (Vv. 40–48)

Following this passage are nine variations on the first two themes and one on the third. With a single exception, found in verse 81, the variations appear in the order of increasing scope, beginning with Alcipe himself: "Resous-toi d'aller chez les Mors" (v. 49); continuing with "le Potentat le plus grand de nos jours" (v. 52) and the "superbes Tyrans du Danube et du Tage" (v. 57); "ces fermes Bastimens" (v. 64); two cities—Troy and Rome:

> On cherche en vain les belles Tours
> Où Paris cacha ses Amours,
> Et d'où ce Féneant vit tant de funerailles.
> Rome n'a rien de son antique orgueil,
> Et le vuide enfermé de ses vieilles murailles
> N'est qu'un affreux objet et qu'un vaste cercueil.
>
> (Vv. 67–72);

the sky: "Et ce beau Ciel, ce lambris azuré" (v. 76); the sun: "Le grand Astre qui l'embellit / Fera sa Tombe de son Lit" (vv. 79–80); the sphere of air beyond the sky but between the earth and the sun: "L'Air ne formera plus ny Gresles, ny Tonnerres" (v. 81); and ending with the "Univers" (v. 82). All these will inevitably perish and, as transitory phenomena, merit Alcipe's scorn or at least that of his immortal soul: "Mais tu dois avecque mespris / Regarder ces petits débris" (vv. 73–74). Aside from the use of climax, the final stanzas possess great closural force, since they contain an unqualified assertion of finality, supported by repetition and parallelism ("ce beau Ciel, ce lambris azuré / Ce Theatre" (vv. 76–77); "ny Gresles, ny Tonnerres" (v. 81);

Le grand Astre qui . . . l'Univers, qui" (vv. 79 and 82); "courir tant de Mers et fleurir tant de Terres" (v. 83); "tomber, tombera" (v. 84).

But poetic closure is not logical conclusiveness: the fact remains that in his direct argumentation the speaker has yet to make his case. Within the explicit terms of the ode, a life of astute epicureanism, removed only from the court, would be a valid alternative to retirement *dans nos Bois*. Moreover, given all eternity to become acquainted with his soul and no compelling reason to establish immediate intimacy, *descente dans soi-même* remains, at least in this context, an elective rather than a mandatory step.

As an exercise in rational persuasion this meandering, loosely argued monologue falls far short of *l'esprit de géométrie*. Still, it possesses remarkable power as rhetoric. Unless this power is illusory, it must stem from sources other than logic. And if this is true, the associative progression may well serve an ulterior purpose.

L'ESPRIT DE FINESSE

One source of the poem's persuasive force, already announced in the developmental transitions, is the rich and cohesive structure of implied metaphors, the various elements of which form two interrelated clusters, one ontological, the other ethical.

Anatomy of the World

Throughout the ode, the speaker meticulously constructs an opposition between two aspects of his—and Alcipe's—world. They are predictable, even trite: appearance and reality. But the combination of ideas gathering about each is paradoxical: with appearances are associated life and being; with reality, death and nothingness. The contrast is manifest on all levels of experience, from the most significant to the most trifling. Appearance, for example, cushions and seduces Alcipe with its yielding delights, its "plaisirs" (v. 20) and "molle douceur" (v. 21). Reality is far poorer: as annihilation, its necessity is both rigorous and rigid, "une Loy" (v. 46). Appearance also includes plenitude: "Ameublement" (v. 25) and its "toile d'or'' (v. 27), in addition to the buildings full of Roman art—fine or practical—implied in verses 70 and 71: "Rome n'a rien de son antique orgueil, / Et le vuide enfermé de ses vieilles murailles." This is, of course, deceptive, for the rich furnishings merely conceal absence and starkness, "le plastre de ta Chambre" (v. 27); likewise, Rome's ancient walls are a "cercueil" (v. 72) enclosing a "vuide" (v. 71). Finally, in the domain of appearance, limits are either unknown or fantastically exaggerated, especially with respect to time and mutability. As popular gods (v. 58), kings seem to avoid all human frailties. So must the idolized ladies of court (or salon) to whom Alcipe's "fole Amour esleve des Autels" (v. 24). Artifices seem equally unshakeable, particularly "ces fermes Bastimens . . . qui jusqu'aux Enfers portent leurs fondemens" (vv. 64 and 66). The most striking symbols of limits evaded are "ces Jardins tousjours vers . . . qui font des Printemps au milieu des Hyvers" (vv. 28 and 30) and, of course, the ancient order of heaven and earth. The "hard law," however, ordains mutability. Its agency, time—"qui tousjours vole" (v. 5), "qui doit tout devorer" (v. 62) "Et qui d'un triste blanc va peindre tes cheveux" (v. 6)—will run out for Alcipe: "Tu vois de prés ta derniere saison" (v. 16). Time will make of us all "pasture aux vers du Monument" (v. 48). Thus kings—and presumably the fine ladies as well—are "fragile[s]" (v. 11); they, too, will suffer, age, and die (v. 12). Time "abatra ces fermes Bastimens" (v. 64), and the season-defying gardens, along with the rest of the external world, will perish: "Sera bruslé des feux dont il est esclairé" (v. 78), and "Sans sçavoir où tomber, tombera quelque jour" (v. 84). All appearance is a "Theatre" (v. 77), where is played out the triple illusion of pliancy, plenitude, and permanence. Inexorably the curtain will fall, leaving of the material world "rien qu'une ombre" (v. 53), "petits débris" (v. 74).

Surviving the catastrophe will be the human soul, man's "propre raison" (v. 18), consigned forever "chez les Mors" (v. 49).

Parameters of Action

Within this ontological frame, Alcipe is a recipient or performer of deeds, potential or actual. As a recipient he consistently undergoes negative experiences; as an agent he may commit positive or negative acts. In any case, what he suffers and what he does finds expression through at least one of three image patterns.

Interiority/exteriority is the first of these. To compound the humiliation of Alcipe's failure at court, the king's favorite mocks Alcipe "dans le Cabinet" (v. 9). In death Alcipe's physical remains (and those of everyone else) will be consumed by worms in a "Tombeau" (v. 60) or a "Monument" (v. 48), whereas his soul is permanently enclosed "où le Cocite / Arrouse des Païs inconnus au Soleil" (v. 41–42). Such well-being as Alcipe can procure in this life consists in liberation and then literal seclusion from the court and its degradations. Thus the speaker urges Alcipe to break out of his gilded "Fers" (v. 13) and use his new freedom to find refuge "dans nos Bois" (v. 1), with the authentic knowledge that is "dans toy-mesme" (v. 15).

Verticality is the second master image in the ethical category. The speaker points out to Alcipe that in his immediate situation he is galled because "ton Rivale monte et tu descens" (v. 8). In the various forms of death, of course, everyone and everything falls: "l'Univers" (v. 83); the Trojan towers: "On cherche en vain les belles Tours / Où Paris cacha ses Amours" (vv. 67–68); these "fermes Bastimens" (v. 64); and all men, whose ultimate destination is the depths of "Enfers" (vv. 41–42, 49, and especially 66). Alcipe has in the past performed various useless and, in the end, humiliating acts: before an indifferent king he has "fléch[i] le genous" (v. 10); in his love for the fine ladies of court or salon, he has "eslev[é] des Autels" (v. 24). The speaker urges Alcipe to break this pattern; but paradoxically, if Alcipe is to regain his superiority, he must begin by making a descent—into himself: "Et descens dans toy-mesme à l'exemple du Sage" (v. 15). Only this, added to complete retirement, will permit him to look "avecque mespris" (v. 73), or *de haut en bas,* on the rubble of a world that is unworthy of him.

Finally, the imagery of horizontal movement supports the various themes just announced. Time advances briskly along a finite track: "Le *cours* de nos ans est borné" (v. 43, emphasis added), "Avant qu'un demy-siecle ait achevé son *cours*" (v. 54, emphasis added). Attempted withdrawal as a means of avoiding death is thus foolish:

C'est en vain que loin des hazars
Où courent les Enfans de Mars,
Nous laissons reposer nos mains et nos courages;

(Vv. 31–33)

but not less foolish than to have "suivy les Rois" (v. 2). In the time remaining, the speaker contends, Alcipe would do best to put a distance between himself and everything false, threatening, and humiliating: "les injustes adorez" (v. 14); "Filis, Amarante et Silvie" (v. 23); the rich furnishings of his room (v. 25); as well as "Jardins tousjours vers" (v. 28). These he must *fuir* or *quitter,* proceeding directly to "nos Bois" (v. 1).

The full import of the speaker's covert argument is now clear. Nothing less than Alcipe's value as a man, his freedom and dignity, are at stake. To remain in a world of seeming pliancy, plenitude, and permanence he would necessarily renounce his *prix,* accepting slavery, falsehood, and humiliation. No compromise is possible. To rehabilitate himself, he must vigorously reassert his independence by total withdrawal to a place of refuge where he can actively confront the rigors, void, and transience of his condition—both individual and generic. This alone will distinguish and thus valorize Alcipe's existence in a universe where all else is vanity.

The chief formal problem posed by this text is its appearance of indeterminacy. Developmentally, the ode is a perfect example of procedure by association, whereas stylistically it is a model of economy and precise thematic schematizing. One might conclude that instead of reinforcing one another, the two formal levels are actually at odds. To dispel this notion, however, requires nothing more than review of the ode's dramatis personae and their relationship.

The speaker is an exponent of philosophical opinions that must be totally—or almost totally—unpalatable to Alcipe. If the latter, after all, did not believe firmly in what the speaker has characterized as the false pliancy, plenitude, and permanence of this world, the ode would have no reason for being. Thus the speaker can allege—and we can believe—that Alcipe idolizes his "infidelle espoir" (v. 3) and is estranged from his "propre raison" (v. 18). By presenting his counterviews sequentially, in a clearcut demonstration, whether inductive or deductive, the speaker might well antagonize the object of his concern and so defeat his own purpose. The alternative—a sententious discourse moving about the periphery of the problem—would at best elicit a polite hearing whose result would be null and void. Rejecting both extremes, Maynard arrived at an ingenious solution, which functionally combines key features of each. On the surface, the speaker proceeds meanderingly and generally, never quite making his case and seeming at last to be carried away by his own rhetorical flourishes. This approach is designed to render Alcipe complacent, to relax his defenses. Caught off guard, Alcipe would be susceptible to artfully indirect suggestion, which is precisely the office of the dialectically complex images. Scattered throughout the developmental structure, these make the poem's disparate details coalesce into the rhetorically significant pattern just described at length. The significance of the patterns would hardly be lost on Alcipe, whose career as a courtier has no doubt taught him much about the perception, synthesis, and interpretation of signs. And, if the calculation is correct, Alcipe's highly developed intuition, sensitivity, and imagination, overwhelmed by the implied analogical arguments, would capitulate and prompt him to retire without delay into the woods, and into himself. Even if he did not withdraw immediately, the foundation would be laid for a future renunciation of the world. In either case, the speaker would realize his long-term objective.

Associative structure rigorized by dispersed symbolism or implied metaphor is extremely common in the French lyric of the early seventeenth century. Further examples by Maynard's contemporaries are Malherbe's "[Alcandre] plaint la captivité de sa maîtresse," Théophile's *La Solitude,* Sigogne's "Galimatias," Tristan L'Hermite's *La Mer,*[9] as well as Saint-Amant's "L'Esté à Rome" and "L'Hyver des Alpes."[10]

1. Smith, p. 139.

2. Guillaume Picot, ed., *Poésie lyrique du moyen âge,* 1:112–14.

3. "Le coq à l'asne fait de jeudi, Xe jour d'aoust, l'an mil cinq cens XXXVII," in Marot's *Oeuvres poètiques,* p. 155.

4. Raphaël du Petit Val, ed., *Recueil de diverses poésies,* p. 84.

5. Schmidt, *Poètes du 16ᵉ siècle,* p. 432. For a detailed treatment of developmental structure and iconology in this sequence, see Ann Elkin Rose, "Du Bellay's *Songe ou Vision.*"

6. La Ceppède, p. 287.

7. Nothing could be more tentative than this hypothesis concerning "traditions" of French associative poetry. The subject is worth a book.

8. Citations of this text refer to François de Maynard, *Poésies,* pp. 161–63.

9. See Robert T. Corum, Jr., "A Reading of Tristan L'Hermite's *La Mer.*"

10. See Corum, *Other Worlds and Other Seas.*

5

Sigogne
Stances ("Cette petite Dame
au visage de cire")

Théophile de Viau
Ode ("Un corbeau devant moy croasse")

Suggestion is but one principle of indeterminate development in the lyric. The other is repetition, which appears in the form of parataxis or catalogue. A complete paratactic structure is tripartite, comprising a generative passage (which may be as long as a stanza or as short as an opening phrase), a set of variations on the themes announced at the outset, and a closural passage[1] like that described in the introduction to the preceding chapter.

The *blason* is the principal sixteenth-century lyric genre in which parataxis was the fundamental structure. A poem by François Sagon typifies the usage. The generating element appears in the opening verse: "Pied de façon à la main comparable."[2] The next forty-two verses describe aspects of the foot with the following syntax:

Pied / relative   (optional repeat)
      prepositional phrase
      adjectival or participal construction.

The elements may be rearranged in any order without affecting the poem's unity and any detail may be omitted or replaced by a synonym, also without important formal consequences, for example:

      Pied amoureux de l'autre sans envie,
      Pied qui peut bien sauver au corps la vie,

77

> Pied mesuré, pied reiglé en son pas,
> Pied qui suyt l'autre en ordre et par compas
> Pied sans lequel un corps captif demeure . . .

The poem closes with a shift of syntax, to the imperative mode, and a logical marker indicating the conclusion (which, by the way, does not follow): "Pied, suis donc l'ordre et triumphe du corps:"

Descriptive unity is only one poetic result of paratactic form, just as loose cataloguing is only one of its devices. Hugues Salel's *blason* on *l'épingle*[3] groups some of the catalogued details into analogous clusters differentiated only by the time of day:

> Tu es au lever et coucher
> De ma maistresse, où approcher
> Je n'ose qu'une foys l'année
> Par toy est toute gouvernée
> La parure du corps joly,
> Premier le front ample et poly
> Quant tu le serres d'une toille
> Se monstre plus cler que l'estoille.
> Apres tu tiens le chaperon . . .

(The paradigm case of "pattern unity" and "temporal framing" in the paratactic lyric is, of course, Villon's *Ballade des dames du temps jadis.* Here a single fact is repeated a dozen times in different ways: Like everything else beautiful, brave, or wise these women *must* disappear. Those in the first stanza belong to classical antiquity; those in the second and third to the immediate past. Within each time frame, however, the order is not rigorous: Héloïse, for example is mentioned before Charlemagne's mother, Berthe au grand pied.)

A BILL OF PARTICULARS

The first parataxis, a spirited satire by Charles Timoléon de Beauxoncles, seigneur de Sigogne, presents a dense, if relatively uncomplicated, version of the form.

> Cette petite Dame au visage de cire,
> Ce manche de cousteau propre à nous faire rire,
> Qui a l'oeil et le port d'un antique rebecq,
> Merite un coup de becq.

4

Elle a la bouche et l'oeil d'une chate malade,
L'Auguste majéste d'une vieille salade;
Sa petite personne et son corps de brochet
8   Resemble un trebuchet.

La voyant pasle et triste en sa blancheur coiffee,
Les Dieux de nos ruisseaux l'estiment une Fee,
Les autres un lapin revenu d'un boüillon
12   Ou bien un papillon.

Le moindre petit vent, pour soulager sa peine,
Comme vent de lutins la porate à la fonteine,
Car elle poise moins, la Nymphe du Jardin,
16   Que son vertugadin.

Je consacre en ces vers sa teste de linotte,
Afin que tous les fols en facent leur marotte
Et veux que de son corps, mistement Damoiseau,
20   On en face un fuzeau.[4]

In the first stanza the speaker furnishes a basis for the catalogue and the closural passage. His procedure is to indicate or imply, through more or less transparent metaphors, aspects of the victim's physical and mental state as a prelude to suggesting what she deserves for being so repugnant. From the beginning he establishes a hostile tone: use of the demonstrative *Cette* isolates and objectifies her, and the term *Dame* is so ironic in context as to suggest the speaker's unmitigated scorn. The first flaw that he cites is her diminutive stature; the second, her unctuous complexion, which is also pale white or pale yellow. He then repeats the idea of puniness with a variation: it is linked with other *défauts pendables*: slenderness, flatness, and hollowness—even rigidity. The judgment clinching the second verse affirms the woman's status as the poet's butt, and ideally the reader's. In the curious verse to follow, he attributes to her the naturally rigid manner or *port,* as well as the *oeil* of an old rebec. Does he mean something akin to the human visual organ, or the rebec's total appearance, or its *état d'esprit?* All three are possible in the French of the early seventeenth century. If the first, then he certainly refers to the pegs that extend laterally from the end of the instrument's fingerboard, in which case he also implies facial misalignment and even exopthalmos, a pathological bulge. (The latter would be quite ironic, of course, since the only convexity granted to the victim is monstrously abnormal.)[5] If he means overall appearance, he refers to the rebec's flatness, slenderness, hollowness, and rigidity. If, finally, he means *état d'esprit*, the speaker suggests a kind of stolid, mindless passivity already implicit in verse 2 and in the reference to the rebec's *port*. Such a constellation of deficiencies, he concludes, deserves punishment. But why a "coup de bec"? Not a gratuitous choice of metaphor, this translates the purely oral (or verbal) aggression of which the poem has consisted so far and *will* consist to the end of its final stanza.

With his scope and procedure established, the speaker now passes to the catalogue proper, which encompasses the next three stanzas. Each one presents a set of variations on one or more of the themes announced in verses 1–4. The order is random and the necessity for any detail minimal. In other words, displacement of any detail or substitution of a "similar" for it would not affect the poem's completeness, integration, or singleness of form.

The first two verses of the second stanza elaborate almost all of the preceding imagery. The speaker first describes the woman's eyes (cf. v. 3) and her mouth (cf. the poet's own, implied in v. 4). These resemble a sick cat's because both produce effluvia that recall viscous rivulets of melting wax. Meanwhile, the wilting ingredients of a "vieille salade" (v. 6) decompose into a similarly vile mess—unless, of course, the *salade* is a *casque*: round, thin, hollow, and metallically cold. More complex is the redundant third verse, which exhibits a literal repetition of the puniness theme found in verse 1, and like the corresponding verse of the first stanza, it presents a dazzling ambiguity. The *brochet* is certainly a pike, and thus both narrow and flat like a rebec or a *manche de cousteau,* but it may also be a faucet quill for a wine bottle, and as such both hollow and relatively stiff. (This would entail a brilliant and gratuitous reversal: for the weapon is to the *manche de cousteau* what the faucet quill is to the wine bottle. The relation of container to thing contained is turned upside down at the further expense of the speaker's victim.) At any rate, he analogizes her small body to a *trébuchet*, or bird trap, small and narrow like the rebec or the *manche de cousteau,* with the latter of which it shares another feature: being an enclosure with only one aperture.

The third stanza extends the themes found in the second. Her pallor and whiteness continue the wax image of verse 1, but her *tristesse* is mysterious, unless it refers to austerity, a probable variant of the rigidity alluded to in verses 1, 2, 3, and 8. That her *blancheur* is *coiffée* poses no problem if the familiar sense of the adjective, "besotted" or "stupid," is taken into account.[6] (The speaker has already suggested in verse 3 that his victim is mindless.) So described, the spectacle of the *Dame* convinces the guttersnipes burlesqued in verse 10 that she is a *fée,* an imaginary woman with magical powers. From the speaker's point of view this judgment is certainly half correct: if she is considered female at all, it can only be in the imagination. Others less fanciful see her for what she is: either like a rabbit returning waterlogged and insipid from a *bouillon* or a butterfly, lightweight, fusiform, and hopelessly thin.

The woman's praeternatural lack of substance, belabored in verses 10 and 12 and indicated in the hollowness imagery of verses 2, 3, and 8 (and possibly 6), is the sole theme developed in the prefinal stanza. Departing radically from the poem's developmental norm (by allowing more than two verses to a theme and by elaborating only one theme in the stanza) the speaker foreshadows the poem's imminent closure. Noteworthy is the reference to her *vertugadin,* a kind of underskirt that serves to puff up a dress. By this image the speaker not only elaborates on his hyperbole but suggests that the woman engages in an unsuccessful effort to mask her *néant.*

The final strophe of this poem is strongly closural. Continuing like its predecessor, to deviate from the norm, the last four lines contain several formal and stylistic novelties: the speaker refers to himself as well as his discourse in verse 17, and the syntax becomes complex, twice admitting use of the subjunctive (vv. 18 and 20). There are, moreover, two markers of finality: the reference to the poem's ultimate purposes and to a double, irreversible metamorphosis. The transformations have an unmistakeable air of the *contrapasso* about them: they seem to punish in the very image of the alleged crime. The speaker has twice suggested that she is mindless and passive (vv. 3 and 9); he now reiterates his charge by referring to her giddiness or "teste de linotte" (v. 17). Accordingly, he intends that her head become the top piece of a traditional fool's scepter, thus the literally blockheaded symbol of mental insufficiency—to be universally recognized and derided as such. Her body falls short of the speaker's ideal of feminine corpulence; but neither does it seem masculine. Instead it is "mistement Damoiseau" (v. 19), or quite like that of an effeminate youth. Being not wholly one or the other, it deserves to be neither; thus the transformation of her fusiform trunk into a *fuseau* is a brilliantly efficient means of desexing an inflexible victim. These wishes, so vehemently expressed, are, of course, the ultimate *coup de bec*.

It is clear from the foregoing that the lyric attains descriptive unity: each of its elements presents an aspect of a substance or its characteristic state. The *contrapasso* does not alter this conclusion. Though it presents a punitive reiteration of that characteristic state, the reiteration is optative, not factual, and in any case it is subsumed under the rubric of "just deserts," which the poet clearly regards as an integral part of the state itself (cf. v. 4).

As with certain consecutive lyrics disrupted in their progress from beginning through middle to end, the satire of Sigogne contains a submerged figurative component that tightens its unity even further.

The speaker's reflections on the *petite Dame* turn on two themes: the concept of the human and, as a corollary, the notion of role, or usefulness. For the speaker, *humanitas* consists of plenitude, vitality, wholesomeness (including formal perfection), as well as consciousness and freedom from nonhuman traits. Only these qualities permit performance of a specifically human function and so justify a specifically human existence.

In the opening stanza the speaker's metaphorical pyrotechnics suggest that none of these norms is even remotely approximated. Instead of plenitude there is the hollowness appropriate to sheath and rebec; wholesomeness is replaced by the pale cast associated with candle wax in addition to the protrusion and uneven alignment necessary in the rebec's system of tuning pegs. The lady's capacity to play a human role is thus diminished to zero, whereas, ironically, each of the objects and substances to which he compares her is not only useful but indispensable to the comfort or safety, pleasure or instruction normally linked with civilized existence. This tension is crucial to what follows, especially in the closural stanza.

In the first two verses of the second stanza, he again compares her with aspects of nonhuman substances that, despite their ravaged or peccant states, once had (and—in the cat's case—may again possess) greater utility than the little lady can ever hope for, at least in her present form. He returns to the "double-bind" procedure of stanza 1 when, in verses 7 and 8, he discounts her for formal similarity to direct and indirect sources of amusement and food.

If, in the rabbit metaphor of the third stanza, he repeats the argumentative procedure of stanza one and the last two verses of stanza two, the same cannot be said of the references to fairy and butterfly. In the first instance he likens the victim to a creature that only seems real and to which tradition has granted the power of transforming others for better or worse; in the second case he draws an analogy between the lady and a creature so attenuated in body as to symbolize the soul, and above all, a being subject to metamorphosis. In both cases there is denial of humanity and substantiality (repeating the symbolism of void and absence in *blancheur*); but there is more importantly a foreshadowing of the victim's closural transformation.

The fourth stanza is, as I intimated earlier, the weakest of the entire poem, but despite its repetition, it does complete a set of four associated but subordinate water images. Just as the *brochet* originates in water, the guttersnipes live in or around it, and the rabbit is brought back from it, so too the *nymphe du jardin* (a cousin of the *fée*) may be taken for solace or even regeneration *à la fontaine*. In other words, what falls short of humanity, what may not adequately perform any specifically human roles (physical, moral, or psychological) may be associated with the virtual, the unformed, and the undifferentiated mass.

The victim's poetic dehumanization accomplished, the speaker wishes to see it confirmed in reality but will not pass up the opportunity to develop a final paradox. Thus the metamorphosis, by which the *teste de linotte* becomes not only a decorative device but a functional constituent of the fool's scepter; and the intersex creature, a sexless object useful in the production of thread. Like the *papillon* she will metamorphose herself; like the *fée* she will metamorphose other substances or objects. In other words, the speaker proposes nothing less than a punishment that will simultaneously rehabilitate the offender, not as a person but in the image of the poem's other nonhuman objects, which are subservient to the social or economic interests of those whom she offends, and to whom she is now useless except as a butt of sarcasm.

APOCALYPSE NOW?

The second example, Théophile de Viau's ode "Un corbeau devant moy croasse," poses far less tractable difficulties of interpretation.

> Un corbeau devant moy croasse,
> Une ombre offusque mes regards,
> Deux bellettes, et deux renards,
> Traversent l'endroit ou je passe:
> 5   Les pieds faillent à mon cheval,
> Mon laquay tombe du haut mal,
> J'entends craqueter le tonnerre,
> Un esprit se presente à moy
> J'oy Charon qui m'apelle à soy,
> 10   Je voy le centre de la terre.
>
> Ce ruisseau remonte en sa source,
> Un boeuf gravit sur un clocher,
> Le sang coule de ce rocher,
> Un aspic s'accouple d'une ourse.
> 15   Sur le haut d'une vieille tour
> Un serpent deschire un vautour,
> Le feu brusle dedans la glace,
> Le Soleil est devenu noir,
> Je voy la Lune qui va cheoir,
> 20   Cet arbre est sorty de sa place.[7]

What immediately strikes the formal analyst of this celebrated lyric is its extreme ambiguity. Just as a case can easily be made for or against the ode's classification as a failed parataxis, so too can one take either side of an argument about the obvious alternative: simultaneous composition. A promising solution resides in a compromise between the two extremes, but like most promising solutions, this one leaves major problems unsolved.

The grounds for regarding the ode as a headless, tailless parataxis are both simple and obvious. There is no generating passage: the catalogue begins immediately, with every unit (but two) consisting of a single verse that expresses the speaker's perception in the following syntax:

subject	/ verb / zero, or		adverbial
(with or without	complement	{	objective
modifier)			infinitive
			etc.

The exceptions are paired verses (3–4 and 15–16) which expand and embroider on the basic pattern, no doubt to counteract monotony by deviating from the strict syntactic norm. Théophile could have displaced them or *re*placed them with "similars." The catalogue ends, as it began, without a marker. There is no closure; the series of spectacles merely stops.

This reading is obviously superficial. It disregards two salient features of the text: (1) a shift in the quality of images beginning with verse 9—from the literal (-seeming) to the mythic; (2) the implications of the term *esprit* in verse 8, which could mean, in this context, "vision" or "fancy."

If indeed that is the sense of *esprit,* then the poem may be a simultaneous composition, not unlike Saint-Amant's caprice, discussed above in chapter 2. In this case the events related in verses 1–7 so provoke the speaker's sensibility that he reacts by hallucinating (vv. 8–20). It would then be the critic's task to clarify the cause-effect, logical, or customary relationships existing between the specifics of the experience and those of the reaction. Appealing as this solution may be, it fails to account for the temporal-causal discontinuity of items in each segment of the poem; nor does it allow for the more likely meaning of *esprit* in this context, to wit: *ghost.*

To avoid these extremes, I suggest that the ode is paratactic—but also possesses temporal framing. It is, in other words, cognate with Villon's *Ballade des dames du temps jadis.* This hypothesis draws strong support from the well-established view that Théophile employed traditional metaphor and iconology throughout the poem. Along with my observations on structure, therefore, I shall present certain obvious equivalencies from sources in Western European myth and folklore as well as the Bible.[8]

The poem opens with a set of variations on the theme of *mauvais augure.* The cry of the perspicacious crow—which menacingly recalls the Latin *cras* (tomorrow)—is the very medium of ill omen, and so generates all that follows. The catalogue serves to make the subject of the omen more precise. The blinding *ombre* symbolizes death, chaos, or the dominance of the irrational. This is echoed in the number two, associated with conflict, antagonism, or opposition and here attached to the ritually unclean weasels and the fraudulent foxes, which cross the innocent speaker's path, thus contributing to an unstable union of opposites. Among its other functions, a horse is expected to give its master timely warning of danger; here, his stumbling may announce future disorder—unless it testifies to his possession by the same destructive forces that threaten the speaker or his world. The idea of disorder presaged is repeated but humanized in the lackey's epileptic seizure. Finally, the repeated thunderclaps suggest divine wrath. Still unclear, however, is whether the foregoing images are actual omens, percepts that the speaker construes as omens, or pure imaginings.

It is at this point that the ambiguity of *esprit* becomes critically important. If the preceding catalogue presents actual omens, then the appearance of a ghost would mark a final and most alarming augury; if, on the other hand, the catalogue presents percepts subjectively construed as omens—or pure imaginings— then *esprit* may do double duty, denoting *vision,* which may, of course, entail the sighting of a ghost.

According to the manner in which the reader resolves the poem's circumstantial and verbal ambiguities, the catalogue that follows relates the fulfillment of omens, the reactive fantasy of a terrified percipient, or the visionary's continued apocalyptic imaginings. In any case, the second set of variations focuses on the dissolution of a world, presented as the inversion of norms. Verses 10 and 11, as Alvin Eustis has pointed out, clearly refer to an earthquake;[9] as such they reflect the lackey's convulsive seizure (v. 7). The stolid, earthbound ox's deliberate climb up the church tower (v. 12) initiates a series of four fitting paradoxes. In the first of these, vital, bodily heat is emitted from an incongruously motionless and chilly source. There follows a denatured, and altogether futile, *mélange* of cruelly destructive species—latent, no doubt, in the crossroads imagery of verse 4. In a second repetition of the dualism theme, the habitual victim of flying carnivores reverses roles with one of them; but if the vulture betokens prophecy and regeneration, its slaughter by an incarnation of death itself must mark the end of time. The imagery of fire and ice, of course, recalls hell. The last three verses assure strong closure, not only by the domination of final, unending darkness (vv. 18 and 19, as prepared in v. 2), but also by an event announced in verse 5, the conclusive dislocation of traditionally stable objects: the moon from its orbit (v. 19) and the tree, symbolizing the world's axis, from its accustomed place.

A final curiosity of this difficult text is that, despite its lack of formal clarity, its unity is apprehensible. Whatever the poem represents, its principle of singleness, completeness, and integration is descriptive. If the poem is "factual," it presents the end of the world in two of its aspects: that of event foreseen and that of foresight fulfilled. If the speaker relates natural events construed as omens and then his reactive vision, the text describes two aspects of his own world: the apperceptive and the imaginative. If, finally, he relates mere visions, the unity of his spirit is at issue. But the ambiguity is inescapable, and with it, the shifting and uncertain grounds for effect.

Catalogue lyrics occur with great frequency in all the poetic *oeuvres* of the period. Among the many rigorized by the devices discussed in this essay are Malherbe's "Sus, debout, la merveille des belles," Saint-Amant's "Les Goinfres," and Tristan L'Hermite's "La Belle Esclave maure."

1. Smith, pp. 98–109.

2. All citations of the *blasons* are to Schmidt, *Poètes du 16e siècle*. The Sagon text appears on pp. 344–45.

3. Schmidt, pp. 350–51.

4. Charles Timoléon de Beauxoncles, seigneur de Sigogne, *Les Oeuvres satyriques complètes du sieur de Sigogne,* ed. Fernand Fleuret and Louis Percaud, p.109.

5. If the eye is, as seems plausible, in the belly of the instrument, the register of the passage shifts from ironic extrusion back to vacuity or hollowness.

6. I am grateful for this detail to Mona Tobin Houston, "Levels of Meaning in Sigogne."

7. Viau, *Oeuvres poétiques,* p. 164.

8. My source is Jean Chevalier and Alain Gheerbrandt, *Dictionnaire des symboles*. For an illuminating treatment of the poet's use of inherited materials see Claire Gaudiani, *The Cabaret Poetry of Théophile de Viau.*

9. Alvin Eustis, "A Deciphering of Théophile's 'Un corbeau devant moy croasse.'"

Afterword
New Anatomies, New Thresholds

Two themes have dominated this essay: the forms of typical lyrics composed during *le premier dix-septième siècle* and their principles of unity. By setting these themes against the broadly delineated background of earlier poetic practice, I have sought above all to enhance the clarity of my argument. Incidentally, however, my juxtapositions have suggested the basis for a new history of the French lyric between 1550 and 1630. Now, to bring the various strands of the discussion together, I shall elaborate briefly on that idea.[1]

From a formal viewpoint, the major poets of mid-sixteenth-century France sought primarily to invest their lyrics with a transparent consecutive unity. Thus they showed an almost invariable preference for two strictly sequential forms, the logical and the temporal. Most often, of course, they succeeded eminently well: the canons and norms of syllogistic, analogy, and induction were scrupulously observed, as were the laws of cause and effect. At times, however, tight succession was ruptured and the poetry complicated by non sequitur, diffuse polemic, self-invalidating comparison, defective induction, or disjointed narrative. In these lyrics no formal device—whether intra- or intertextual—offsets the loss of consecutive unity. Meanwhile the major poets occasionally joined their colleagues outside the mainstream and employed repetitive or associative structures, content, it would appear, with loosely descriptive or iterative results.

Undertaken during the very late sixteenth century, La Ceppède's *Théorèmes* typify the second phase, in which all "irregularities" were preempted by the poem's sequential designs both local and global. In this work didactic, rather than consecutive, unity is the poetic end, a fact which determined the selection and hierarchizing of expository structures. Specifically, the Ignatian meditative sequence is fundamental and is subserved by a temporal series whose matter is the Passion of Christ. Although a small number of the cycle's disrupted, indeterminate and hybrid sonnets prove, on close study, to be "free-floating," the majority contribute almost routinely to the progressive movement of the speaker's thought and feeling or their occasions and pretexts.[2]

During the third and final stage, consecutive unity ceased to be the primary—or even a contributory— end of lyric form. Description, instruction, and reiteration supplanted it, but in a wholly unforeseeable way. Rather than simply substitute parataxis and association (or fable, exemplum, allegory, and parable) for the prevailing structure, Malherbe, Saint-Amant, Théophile, and others ingeniously adapted the inherited repertory. The adaptation involved two simultaneous procedures. The poet initiated (and normally completed) strict serial development, but broke it up with paratactic or associative digressions; or he omitted cause-effect links or logical markers. At the same time, he exploited dispersed symbolism or implied metaphor as integral, if inconspicuous, features of the speaker's thought. This "submerged" action assures the poem's nonconsecutive unity by transforming *disjecta membra* into elements of proof, instances of a repeating situational or episodic pattern, or aspects of a described entity or state. Concurrently with this shift of poetics, unity in purely paratactic or associative poetry was rigorized to an unprecedented degree by the use of the same devices: witness the achievements of Maynard, Sigogne, and Théophile de Viau, among others.

To transcend the limits of the foregoing schematism—that is, to produce a *narrative* history of French lyric forms between 1550 and 1630, will demand further study on a massive scale. The general and special poetic causes of change must be uncovered

and related. So, too, must the *extra*poetic causes, whether proxi-
mate (in literary theory, for example) or remote (as in the relationship of poet to audience).[3] Nor can biographical data be ig-
nored, whenever they bear directly on the sources and origins of
works. But logically prior to all historical studies (except, of
course, the establishment and annotation of texts) is the understanding of these texts as artistic wholes. Such critical inquiry
has long been under way for the achievements of the Pléiade and
its immediate successors, as well as Jean de La Ceppède; but it
has only begun for the perplexing lyrics of Malherbe and his
younger contemporaries. This situation is due, as I have suggested, to a scarcity of conceptual and methodological frame-
works broad enough, differential enough, and inductive enough
for practical critics to proceed, sure of attaining comprehensive
and rigorous results. The method just set forth and illustrated—
its focus fixed on the subsumptive relations of purpose, object,
manner, and means—is but one step in the required direction.
Though subject, like any other approach, to refinement for
greater validity or dismissal in favor of a more adequate system,
mine will have served its purpose if it inclines, encourages, or
provokes the reader to study the lyrics of early seventeenth-
century France as, ultimately, they *must* be studied: for their
own sake and in their own nature.

1. See R. S. Crane, *Critical and Historical Principles of Literary History*, for
the criteria employed in these remarks.

2. Terence Cave has suggested to me that Du Bartas's *La Sepmaine Saincte*
also falls into this category, because its organization is based on the conventional procession of days.

3. See Henri Lafay, *La Poésie française du premier dix-septième siècle*, for
the first serious research into this area.

Appendix
The Odes of Malherbe Reconsidered

Higher, Hidden Order contains no analysis of the developmental principles operative in Malherbe's six completed odes. Hence, to assure methodological consistency between *Higher, Hidden Order* and this, its sequel, I shall now account as succinctly as possible for the explicit progression of each ode, and for its unity.

A LA REINE SUR SA BIEN-VENÜE EN FRANCE

Beginning logically, but soon shifting to nonconsecutive development, Malherbe's first completed ode establishes a pattern for the entire series of six.

In the first section, addressed to the people of France (or, more specifically, perhaps, to the citizens of Aix-en-Provence), the poet urges them to crown the newcomer with flowers. Simultaneously, he hopes that national grief will end and that recent civil disturbances will be suppressed (stanza 1). If these wishes are granted, he implies, there will be civil harmony, and—despite the crepe hangers—France will long endure (stanza 2). The reason for this guarded optimism is the arrival of Marie de Médicis, the unsurpassed beauty who is now the king's bride (stanza 3). Her beauty exceeds that of Venus in search of a new lover, or Aurora when she rises (stanza 4). Though supremely meritorious by birth, she is not vain; her virtues, incidentally, include eloquence and purity (stanza 5). So marvelous is she that Neptune held her captive for ten days during her transit from Florence (stanzas 6 and 7). Summing up this *éloge,* the poet asserts that however overblown praises of Marie may seem, they still fall short of the truth (stanza 8).

The next five stanzas depart from the logical model to present variations on a theme already announced in the first twenty verses: Marie's beneficial effects on France. They include the ending of "nos tenebres, et nos hyvers"[1] (v. 84), the renewal of cities, the permanent extirpation of civil strife (stanza 10), as well as the birth of a Dauphin, who, while still young, will conquer the world by force or by charm (stanzas 11 and 12). Finally, the queen will so enchant the king that he will stop risking his life—and hence the peace and stability of the nation—in battle (stanza 13).

There follows a seven-stanza digression on the king's thirst for glory, an admirable, if dangerous, trait even in one already basking in universal admiration (stanza 14). He should content himself with what he has already accomplished (and with wooing the queen) rather than tempt fate by seeking out further dangers (stanza 15). If he must congratulate himself, let it be for the pleasure that the queen gives him (stanza 16). The next three stanzas are *redites* of preceding material: fear that Henri's commitment to wage war personally will undo what he has achieved (stanza 17); an argument against tempting fate, with an analogy to the legend of Achilles (stanza 18); a reminder that the Parcae are fickle (stanza 19); and a concession that unconquered territory presents Henri IV with great—even irresistible—temptations; he should however, delegate the risks to others (stanza 20).

Repeating the theme already expressed in stanza 13 (that Marie's charms will keep the king at home), the poet adds that the rebels should be punished with hard labor (stanza 21). The poem ends on an evocation of those proxies (stanzas 22 and 23).

Implied metaphor unites the various segments of the poem. Throughout the text the poet compares the queen and king to such mythical couples as Peleus and Thetis or Venus and Anchises. From such a union of goddess or demigoddess and hero a son is born—Achilles in one case, Aeneas in the other. It is the son's destiny, incidentally, to outshine his father. Meanwhile the couple separates because of male pride—Anchises' indiscreet boast of having made love to Venus, and Peleus's selfish effort to prevent Thetis from rendering the infant Achilles invulnerable. If, however, the queen succeeds in cooling Henri's pride, this royal couple will not be separated by a fate angered at the king's incessant risk-taking.[2] Thus the ode possesses iterative unity of a special sort: whereas the protagonists reenact the character and actions of a preexistent literary model, they will prove themselves superior to their predecessors in it and thereby establish a new standard of excellence, if (and only if) they reverse the tragic component of that model.

SUR L'ATTENTAT COMMIS EN LA PERSONNE DE SA MAJESTÉ LE 19 DE DECEMBRE 1605

Malherbe's second ode consists of four tight sequential blocks—three of them logical, one narrative. The articulations between them, however, are virtually nonexistent; and but for a shared (if at times peripheral) anguish occasioned by the threat of civil disorder, the various parts of the poem seem unfocused.

The first block consists of stanzas 1 and 2, in which the poet rhetorically asks future generations how they will read or hear of present-day events without shame, for this age is marked by such a decline from past courage that its crimes surpass the worst ever committed in Africa.

Without transition of any sort, the poet then shifts to praise of Henri IV: the greatest of kings, world-famous, and deserving of worship after God Himself (stanza 3). So great is he, the poet continues, that if ineligible by birth to rule France, he would certainly have been elected to that office (stanza 4). Nevertheless his subjects are ungrateful and violent, always in revolt against him (stanza 5). As proof, one need only consider the two recent attempts on Henri IV's life (stanza 6).

Again, without ligament to the preceding material, the poet changes the subject. Apostrophizing the sun, he demands to know why it did not plunge France into darkness by returning to the eastern horizon during the most recent *attentat* (stanza 7). He then reproaches the sun further as ignorant, insensitive, and unfree or governed by outside forces (stanza 8). Reversing himself, the poet calls his statements irrational and admits that the assassin was too intelligent to attempt anything unless the sun had already set in the west (stanza 9).

In the third section the poet passes without warning to a narration of the Seine god's flight—and that of his nymphs—at the time of the most recent attempt on the king's life (stanza 10). Motivated by fear of civil chaos (stanza 11), they may now return, for the king is safe (stanza 12) and the traitors will be punished (stanza 13).

The final section, also unprepared, is an address to the genius presiding over France's destiny. First the poet declares that the genius's good works are unforgettable (stanza 14), especially the aid given to the king's all-too-human bodyguards, who otherwise would not have spotted the would-be assassin in time (stanza 15). He then reminds the good demon that Henri IV is indispensable to the well-being of France: as a refuge and aid to the innocent (stanza 16) and as a scourge of the guilty (stanza 17). If, therefore, the genius is to fulfill its mission, it must defend him, preserve and defend the queen (stanzas 18–19), safeguard their marriage (stanza 20), and make it fertile (stanza 21). Above all, it must enable the Dauphin to defend the realm and conquer hostile Spain within his parents' lifetime (stanza 22).

To compensate for the consecutive unity that this ode obviously lacks, Malherbe employed both implied allusion—as in the first of the six encomiastic poems—and, for the first time, a network of symbolic images. The former liken contemporary France to the mythical and violent age of iron, and the king to Zeus at war with the giants. A double, interlocking pattern is thus established to synthesize the various segments. Deeply pessimistic, however, the poet argues that only by divine intervention can the House of Navarre—here, the force of light—mobilize itself to defeat rebellious subjects and foreign enemies (associated throughout with darkness and frenetic movement). On fulfillment of the second pattern, of course, depends reversal of the first, and a return to the age of gold.[3]

AU FEU ROY SUR L'HEUREUX SUCCEZ DU VOYAGE DE SEDAN

In Malherbe's third ode there is a group of sequential passages—both logical and narrative—linked by association in one instance and culminating in a coda. On the local level the poem *tends* toward consecutive unity, though overall it falls short of that condition.

The first four stanzas form one discursive block, in which the poet expresses relief at the advent of peace (stanza 1), explaining that rebellious Sedan surrendered as soon as Henri IV set out to put it down (stanza 2); he then justifies the tone of stanza 1 by disclosing that a bloodbath had been expected (stanza 3), but Henri's skill averted this (stanza 4).

A second discursive block follows, connected with the preceding segment by the association of similars. Stanzas 5–8 present a complete proportional analogy in which Henri IV is likened in his forcefulness to a rampaging river swollen with melted snow. The king, however, has two qualities not attributable to the flood: self-control (v. 54) and its corollary, a sweet-natured reaction to surrender following harsh resistance.

Stanza 9 is closural, returning with great intensity to the theme of stanza 1, which the speaker recasts as an unqualified dismissal of "vaines chimeres" (v. 81), which have plagued the nation with hatred, rancor, and suspicion until Henri IV showed his strength and secured the country.

Instead of ending here, however, the poem continues, with all the prior material motivating further discursive activity. Henri, argues the poet, is superhuman (stanza 10), having averted a national tragedy (stanza 11). In addition, he is so lucid and completes his projects with such efficacy that Fortune loves to serve him and is angered when not employed by the French sovereign (stanza 12). Henri IV, therefore, should continue to act (stanza 13). The poet then concedes that the as-yet-unconceived *dauphin* is expected to conquer the Levant (stanza 14), but while awaiting that event, why should Henri not dispose of France's troublesome neighbors (stanza 15)? The poet then presents three arguments in favor of immediate action. Those enemies protected by the Alps will miraculously lose their geographical shield—as soon as the mountains know that Henri has launched an attack (stanza 16). Furthermore, a generation of young soldiers are burning to win glory for their king; what a waste it would be if the king left them idle (stanza 17). Finally, the troublemaking neighbors, symbolized by their rivers, are losing their courage and have therefore become vulnerable (stanza

18). The poet then winds his argument up with a resumptive exhortation to march and win (stanza 19).

The coda follows, articulated by a locative to the passage of praise and advice: if and when Henri defeats Milan (stanza 19), the poet will be there (stanza 20), commending the king. Typically, the final stanzas connect adulation of the king with self-adulation, but atypically, the coda proceeds in a logical manner. First, the poet argues that the king will be pleased to hear his praises sung, all the more so because it is only through poetry that man escapes mortality (stanza 21); for Henri this is particularly true: the subject of Malherbe's *éloges* will *never* be forgotten or disvalued (stanza 22).

Tightly argued as it may be in its various parts, the ode is not consecutively unified. It falls into three distinct sections without focus or subordination on the explicit, argumentative level. Throughout the ode, however, the poet implicitly analogizes Henri IV to Hercules and Theseus,[4] showing that in respect to merit, the king reenacts the heroes' lives, while—free from their defects—he makes none of their fatal errors. Reinforcing this variant of iterative unity is an extensive system of dispersed symbols, similar to those found in other odes, in which the king is associated with light and elevation whereas his rivals appear on a reduced scale or under a shadow, and his enemies are cast into abysmal darkness.[5]

A MONSEIGNEUR LE DUC DE BELLEGARDE,
GRAND ESCUYER DE FRANCE

The centerpiece of the fourth ode is a parataxis, flanked by logical developments. The formal effects of this—and the almost complete absence of transition—are entirely predictable.

The overture of the ode is unusually long, self-reflexive, and ingeniously argued. The poet reproaches himself for failing to write in praise of his celebrated patron, Bellegarde (stanza 1). The poet cannot, after all, be purer than the Muses, who decline to flatter but never let great services go unsung (stanza 2). *A fortiori,* virtue—the most valuable product of studying poetry—despises ingratitude more than any other vice; no acknowledgment of virtue, moreover, is longer loved than a pleasing poem (stanza 3). The poet closes this section of the work by swearing that *his* praises are unforgettable. If indeed he fails to make the world love Bellegarde's glory as much as Bellegarde loves the poet's verse, then the promise of Parnasse is illusory (stanza 4).

Without transition the poet passes to a second discursive tack: a complete proportional analogy in which he likens himself, hesitating among Bellegarde's qualities, to a man paralyzed by indecision as he tries to compose a garland in an abundant and richly varied garden (stanzas 5 and 6).

The next twelve stanzas constitute a set of variations on the theme of Bellegarde's greatness. Members of the patron's house have always held positions of responsibility (stanza 7) and their military service has upheld the crown (stanza 8). The poet then rejects discussion of ancestry as degrading: Bellegarde shines by his own, not reflected, glory (stanza 9). Even Envy praises him (stanza 10). A great military horseman (stanza 11), Bellegarde was the handsome escort who enchanted the ravishing Marie de Médicis when she came to France from Italy (stanza 12). Even the nymphs along the way could not decide which of the two was divine (stanza 13). Then without ado the poet returns to the question of military virtue (stanza 14). Though unprecedented, Achilles' good looks and social graces would never have assured his immortality; he had to vanquish Troy singlehandedly for fame (stanzas 15 and 16). Likewise, Bellegarde earned undying reknown through valor (stanza 17). The poet lauds Bellegarde's incorruptible loyalty and courage during recent upheavals (stanza 18). A proportional analogy repeats this praise (stanzas 19 and 20). The king has always had Bellegarde's help, the poet concludes (stanzas 21 and 22).

Then the poet suddenly announces that he must stop. His explanation is that to continue might anger Bellegarde (stanza 23). To close the ode, the poet expresses hope that Bellegarde will be pleased by the poem (stanza 24) and that he and his brother Termes may acquire further glory (stanzas 25 and 26).

If consecutive unity is absent from this text, the far-flung digression and the curious repetitions coalesce as the referent of a metaphor whose analogue is the Gemini: Castor and Pollux.[6] In contrast with the protagonists of preceding odes, however, Bellegarde and Termes—though tall, handsome, and brilliant[7]—will never equal (let alone surpass) their mythic counterparts—at least in fame. To accomplish that would require the impossible: an apotheosis. Thus perhaps did Malherbe distinguish between kings and their servants.

A LA REYNE MERE SUR LES HEUREUX SUCCEZ DE SA REGENCE

Malherbe's briefest ode begins as a loose but fundamentally logical development. Shortly after a closural passage, however, it shifts to the associative mode, and ends with a coda.

In the first stanza the poet exhorts Fame to sing Marie's praises everywhere. His reasons appear in two parataxes which follow. Comprising stanzas 2 and 3, the first set of variations focuses on grounds for fear at the beginning of the regency: the murder of Henri IV and the resultant threat of civil disorder with grave international effects. The second set of variations (stanzas 4 and 5) shows that those fears were not realized: there has been internal calm for almost four months and a crucial military victory at Juliers. Transition from the subsection on fear to that on happier realities is assured by the logical marker "toutesfois." In a final set of variations (stanzas 6 and 7) the poet argues that Marie's brilliant administrative record entitles her to apotheosis and control over the rising and setting of the sun. The sense of closure is very strong in these lines thanks to the device of "coming

full circle." The "miracles" of her regency (v. 54) have placed Marie
on an equal footing with her husband, "de qui la gloire / Fut un
merveille à nos yeux" (vv. 11–12, emphasis mine). The appearance of a
"Demon" (v. 62), analogous to "Fame" (v. 1), whose office it is to
disseminate knowledge of the queen's deeds (vv. 62 ff) reinforces this
effect.

Rather than end—and attain consecutive unity—at line 70, the ode
continues, with the principle of suggestion governing the passage from
one part to another. The eighth stanza initially expresses concern that
good fortune will not continue, and closes on a distinct note of fear:
chance may indeed reverse the happy trend completely. Though stanza
8 does contain one logical marker, "Mais si . . . " (v. 77), the transition from stanza 7 is due mainly to the continuity of verbal action (an
address to Marie, begun in stanza 6). From anxiety about reversal, the
poet passes associatively in stanza 9 to the means of avoiding it. He
recommends ending violence and finding better uses for French
vaillance. The theme of ill will, which appears at the end of the ninth
stanza, prompts the general observation of stanza 10: that internal
discord is the downfall of states. By negative suggestion, strife recalls
peace; hence stanza 11, where the poet evokes the abundance, happiness, and political stability resulting from political calm and order.
This mental and verbal careening ends with a prediction of popular
obedience and safety as the prelude to a new age of gold (stanza 12).

The last three stanzas close the second part of the ode with the
promise that if successful, Marie will receive the Muses' praise. The
poet's work in this calling is, of course, acknowledged as unsurpassed;
he is, in fact, ranked among the "trois ou quatre seulement" (v. 148)
whose encomiastic creations will last forever. The device of "coming
full circle" occurs again, serving to link the coda not only with stanzas
of the second movement but also with those of the first. Thus reappear
terms or images pertaining to royal or heroic headgear, such as
couronne (v. 145, cf. vv. 44 and 109); time and eternity (v. 150, cf. vv.
57 and 118–20); elevation (v. 131, cf. vv. 39–40, 47, and 115), and the
miraculous (v. 129, cf. vv. 12 and 54), as well as supernatural beings
like the *muses* who publicize human success (v. 121, cf. vv. 1 and 62).

That the ode lacks consecutive unity is clear enough: it falls into two
distinct sections, one complete, single, and logically integrated, the
other dispersed and associative. The coda may yoke the two parts
together but it cannot make them cohere. That is the function of the
allusive metaphor in which the speaker systematically likens Marie to
Semiramis[8] and the spatial vocabulary in whose terms he defines
Marie's role as guide, hierarchizer, suppressor of evil, and repressor of
inappropriate conduct.[9] The result, again, is an iternative unity, for
Marie recapitulates (to her greater glory) the *grandes lignes* of the
Assyrian queen's biography and, in a new setting, reenacts her political
rôle.

POUR LE ROY ALLANT CHASTIER LA REBELLION DES
ROCHELOIS ET CHASSER LES ANGLOIS QUI EN LEUR
FAVEUR ESTOIENT DESCENDUS EN L'ISLE DE RÉ

Malherbe's sixth and final ode closely resembles the fifth—discursive at first but after a closural passage shifting to a series of disgressions, some associative, others paratactic.

The first ten quatrains are fundamentally logical. The poet urges the king to destroy the rebels (stanzas 1 and 2 and the final lines of 3), then justifies his exhortation (stanzas 3–7) before repeating the plea and giving a final assurance that Louis XIII is as strong as the Protestants are weak. Within this argumentative framework, however, the poet liberally employs parataxis to drive his imperatives home and to martial his supporting evidence. Stanzas 1 and 2 (as well as the last two verses of stanza 3) are virtually synonymous, a set of variations on the theme of Louis as Hercules the Hydra-Slayer. The first two verses of stanza 3 and the next four quatrains present a rationale for action. The parts, which could be arranged in any order or replaced by similars, stress the rebels' faults and misdeeds: "infidelle malice" (v. 9), a century-long history of "brutales manies" (v. 15), the unsurpassed "inhumanité" they manifest today (v. 19), and their devastating effect on the economy (vv. 21–24), in addition to a uniquely repugnant fusion of civil and religious impiety (vv. 25–28). In stanza 8 the imperatives of stanzas 1, 2, and 3 are repeated four times (in three cases without conjunction). The Protestants' weakness is then portrayed in a series of variations on the theme of *précautions inutiles*: their complex and laborious efforts at defense will be futile, because the king's "cause est la cause de Dieu" (v. 38).

Then by double association the poet passes to praise of Richelieu, whose name is rimed with that of the diety (vv. 38 and 40) and who, appropriately enough, is the king's main support here below. The prelate's qualities are catalogued, like the misdeeds of the Protestants, in random order: committed to spreading Louis's *grandeur* (stanza 11), he is single-minded (stanza 12), sharp of perception and intellect, as well as magnanimous, bold, and skillful (stanza 13). The next quatrains close the Richelieu digression with a removal of earlier commands and a *pointe* (that nothing less than a man of Richelieu's stature would adequately reward the king's piety). Characteristically, however, Malherbe uses the closural passage to link the digression with the preceding materials, stating that with Richelieu's aid, Louis need not delay his anti-Protestant initiative (vv. 59–60).

By an associative leap from one cause (Richelieu) to a similar the poet now presents a vision of victory personified. The opening stanzas in this section (16–18) describe the goddess—her place and dress (v. 63), her speech inviting the king to march (vv. 66–68), her bearing and confidence (vv. 69–72). By a second associative shift (from present and future historical situations to similars in classical myth) the poet compares Louis to Zeus and the Protestants to the giants who besieged

Olympus. Thanks to Victory, the giants failed (so, too, will the Protestants) and Zeus triumphed (as will Louis). The poet then imagines in stanzas 23 to 25 that the Protestants have drawn the same analogy. Recognizing their fate they should surrender, and their English allies flee, knowing the punishments that may await them if they resist. Neptune will aid Louis in his military effort (stanzas 26–28). In a return to logical order the poet then enumerates the direct effect of victory: greater respect for the French the world over (stanza 29).

The next ten stanzas represent another departure from the general drift of the ode. There the poet expresses his personal regret that, being old, he cannot collaborate materially in the triumph (stanza 30). He will, therefore, miss the incomparable honor of dying in the king's service (stanzas 31 and 32). From an emphatic repetition of his melancholy (stanzas 33–35), he passes by the opposition of mind and body to confidence in his power to serve Louis as a poet (stanza 35). There follow four stanzas of variations on the theme of the poet's incomparable gifts, which, divinely acquired at birth and still valid, permit him to weave a laurel wreath of words for the sovereign. The final stanza, which returns to the idea of international fame (originating in the Richelieu digression and continued in the Victory digression), brings the poem almost full circle.

Like the fifth ode, the sixth is devoid of consecutive unity. My analysis of the imagery shows, however, that the scattered fragments of Malherbe's address to the king are drawn into a coherent totality. First the interests of the crown are consistently and pervasively associated with light, elevation, order, and then plenum; by contrast, the interests of his adversaries are associated with darkness, abasement of the lofty, emergence of what ought to lie hidden, and the emptying of what should remain full, as well as the imposition of limits on that which should be infinite. Second, the king appears—in quite similar terms—as a dependent: first, on Richelieu's lucidity and moral stature, which will enable Louis to preside over an orderly and prosperous realm; and second, on Malherbe's poetic illumination and creative vigor, which will assure his attainment of worldwide, eternal fame as a personage of encomiastic literature.[10] In short, Malherbe pulls the various fragments of the lyric together as aspects of the king's being and becoming, potentiality and actuality. Alone among the six poems, the final ode attains descriptive unity.

From the foregoing it is now clear that the six odes of Malherbe include disrupted and diffused sequences but attain iterative or descriptive unity, thanks to implied metaphor or dispersed symbolism. (What distinguishes the Malherbian ode from its competitors, it appears, is the extreme rigor of certain logical passages, found most frequently at the beginning of the text.) Far from being formally unique or even extraordinary, then, Malherbe's odes may stand as specimens of early seventeenth-century French poetic.

1. All citations of the odes refer to Malherbe, *Oeuvres poétiques*, ed. Fromilhague and Lebègue.

2. Rubin, *Higher, Hidden Order*, pp. 29–46.

3. Ibid., pp. 45–50.

4. Ibid., pp. 58–63.

5. Ibid., pp. 63–67.

6. Ibid., pp. 77–80.

7. Ibid., pp. 80–82.

8. Ibid., pp. 88–90.

9. Ibid., pp. 90–93.

10. Ibid., pp. 101–7.

Bibliography

PRIMARY SOURCES

La Ceppède, Jean de. *Les Théorèmes sur le sacré mystère de nostre rédemption*. Toulouse, 1613–22. Reprint. Preface by Jean Rousset. Travaux de l'humanisme et Renaissance 80. Geneva: Droz, 1966.

Malherbe, François de. *Oeuvres poétiques*. Edited by René Fromilhague and Raymond Lebègue. 2 vols. Paris: Société d'édition "Les Belles Lettres," 1968.

Marot, Clément. *Oeuvres poétiques*. Edited by C. A. Mayer. London: Athlone Press, 1962.

Maynard, François de. *Poésies*. Edited by Ferdinand Gohin. Paris: Garnier, 1927.

New English Bible, The. Oxford: Oxford University Press; Cambridge: At the University Press, 1970.

Ovid. *Heroides and Amores*. Translated by Grant Showerman. Loeb Classical Library. London and New York: Heinemann and Putnam, 1925.

Ovid. *Metamorphoses*. Translated by Frank Justus Miller. Loeb Classical Library. Cambridge: Harvard University Press; London: Heinemann, 1946.

Petit Val, Raphaël de, ed. *Recueil de diverses poésies*. Paris: Raphaël du Petit Val. 1597.

Picot, Guillaume, ed. *Poésie lyrique du moyen âge*. 2 vols. Paris: Larousse, 1963.

Ronsard, Pierre de. *Les Amours*. Edited by Henri Weber and Catherine Weber. Paris: Garnier, 1963.

————. *Oeuvres complètes.* Edited by Paul Laumonier. Vol. 2. Paris: Lemerre, 1914.

Saint-Amant. *Oeuvres.* Edited by Jean Lagny. 4 vols. Paris: Didier, 1967–71.

Schmidt, Albert-Marie, ed. *Poètes du 16ᵉ siècle.* Paris: Gallimard, 1953.

Sigogne, Charles Timoléon de Beauxoncles, seigneur de. *Les Oeuvres satyriques complètes du sieur de Signogne.* Edited by Fernand Fleuret et Louis Percaud. Paris: Bibliothèque des Curieux, 1920.

Tristan L'Hermite. *Les Amours et autres poésies choisies.* Edited by Pierre Camo. Paris: Garnier, 1925.

————. *Poésies.* Edited by P. A. Wadsworth. Paris: Seghers, 1962.

————. *Les Vers héroïques.* Edited by Catherine M. Grisé. Geneva: Droz, 1967.

Vermeil, Abraham de. *Poésies.* Edited by Henri Lafay. Geneva: Droz, 1976.

Viau, Théophile de. *Oeuvres poétiques.* Edited by Jeanne Streicher. 2 vols. Geneva and Lille: Droz and Giard, 1951–58.

Virgil. *Virgil I.* Edited and translated by H. R. Fairclough. Loeb Classical Library. Cambridge: Harvard University Press; London, William Heinemann, 1967.

GENERAL POETICS, POETICS OF THE LYRIC,
AND METHODOLOGY

Brooks, Cleanth. *The Well-Wrought Urn.* New York: Harcourt Brace, 1947.

Crane, R. S. *Critical and Historical Principles of Literary History.* Chicago: University of Chicago Press, 1971.

————. *The Languages of Criticism and the Structure of Poetry.* Toronto: University of Toronto Press, 1953.

Olson, Elder. *On Value Judgments in the Arts and Other Essays.* Chicago: University of Chicago Press, 1976.

————. *The Poetry of Dylan Thomas.* Chicago: University of Chicago Press, 1954.

————. *Tragedy and the Theory of Drama.* Detroit: Wayne State University Press, 1961.

Pasco, Allan H. "A Topography of Allusion." Lecture delivered at the University of Virginia, 4 November 1974.

Rubin, David Lee. *Higher, Hidden Order: Design and Meaning in the Odes of Malherbe.* University of North Carolina Studies in Romance Languages and Literatures 117. Chapel Hill: University of North Carolina Press, 1972.

Smith, Barbara Herrnstein. *Poetic Closure: A Study of How Poems End*. Chicago: University of Chicago Press, 1968.

Weinberg, Bernard. *The Limits of Symbolism*. Chicago: University of Chicago Press, 1966.

WORKS CONSULTED

Abraham, C. K. *Enfin Malherbe*. Lexington: University of Kentucky Press, 1971.

Buffum, Imbrie. *Studies in the Baroque from Montaigne to Rotrou*. New Haven: Yale University Press, 1957.

Cave, Terrence C. *The Cornucopian Text: Problems of Writing in the French Renaissance*. Oxford: Clarendon Press, 1979.

————. *Devotional Poetry in France ca. 1570–1613*. Cambridge: At the University Press, 1968.

Chevalier, Jean, and Gheerbrandt, Alain. *Dictionnaire des symboles*. Paris: Laffont, 1969.

Corum, Robert T., Jr. *Other Worlds and Other Seas*. Lexington: French Forum Monographs, 1979.

————. "A Reading of Tristan L'Hermite's *La Mer*." *Papers on French Seventeenth-Century Literature* 9 (1978): 11–28.

Cotgrave, Randle. *A Dictionarie of the French and English Tongues*. London, 1611. Reprint. Columbia: University of South Carolina Press, 1950.

Eustis, Alvin. "A Deciphering of Théophile's 'Un corbeau devant moy croasse.'" *L'Esprit Créateur*, in press.

Fromilhague, René. *Malherbe: Technique et création poétique*. Paris: Colin, 1954.

Gaudiani, Claire. *The Cabaret Poetry of Théophile de Viau: Texts and Traditions*. Etudes Littéraires Françaises. Tübingen: Gunter Narr Verlag; Paris: Editions Jean-Michel Place, forthcoming.

Hafer, Nancy W. "The Art of Metaphor in La Ceppède's *Théorèmes* of 1613." Ph.D. dissertation, University of Virginia, 1975.

————. "Developmental Patterns in La Ceppède's *Théorèmes*." *Papers on French Seventeenth-Century Literature* 7 (1977): 13–34.

Hallyn, Fernand. *Formes métaphoriques dans la poésie lyrique de l'âge baroque en France*. Geneva: Droz, 1975.

Houston, Mona Tobin. "Levels of Meaning in Sigogne." Seminar on French Satirical Poetry of the Early Seventeenth Century, Modern Language Association Convention, Chicago, 28 December 1973.

Hubert, Judd D. "Myth and Status: Malherbe's Swan Song." *Yale French Studies* 49 (1973): 132–42.

Ingold, Catherine. "Form and Value in the Poetry of Saint-Amant. Ph.D. dissertation, University of Virginia, 1978.

Lafay, Henri. *La Poésie française du premier dix-septième siècle.* Paris: Nizet, 1976.

Lanson, Gustave. *Histoire de la littérature française.* 1894. Reprint. Paris: Hachette, 1951.

Lapp, John C. *The Brazen Tower.* Stanford Studies in French and Italian Literature 7. Saratoga, Calif.: Anma Libri, 1977.

Lawrence, Francis L. "Saint-Amant's 'L'Hyver des Alpes,' a Structural Analysis." *Romanic Review* 68 (1977): 247–53.

Leiner, Wolfgang. "'Le Promenoir des deux amans,' lecture d'un poème de Tristan L'Hermite." *Papers on French Seventeenth-Century Literature* 9 (1978): 29–49.

Martz, Louis L. *The Poetry of Meditation.* New Haven: Yale University Press, 1954.

Mourgues, Odette de. *Metaphysical, Baroque, and Précieux Poetry.* Oxford: Clarendon Press, 1953.

Nelson, Lowry. *Baroque Lyric Poetry.* New Haven: Yale University Press, 1961.

Nicolich, Robert. "The Baroque Dilemma: Some Recent French Mannerist and Baroque Criticism." *Oeuvres et Critiques* 1 (1976): 21–36.

Pederson, John. *Images et figures dans la poésie française de l'âge baroque.* Copenhagen: Akademisk Forlag, 1974.

Rose, Ann Elkin. "Du Bellay's *Songe ou Vision*: A Structural and Stylistic Analysis." Master's thesis, University of Virginia, 1975.

Rousset, Jean. *La Littérature de l'âge baroque en France.* Paris: Corti, 1954.

Rubin, David Lee. "Malherbe and the Mannerist Hypothesis: Structure in the Major Poems, 1600–1628." *Papers on French Seventeenth-Century Literature* 1 (1973): 41–50.

———. "Mannerism and Love: The Sonnets of Abraham de Vermeil." *L'Esprit Créateur* 6 (1966): 253–63.

Schevill, Rudolph. *Ovid and the Renaissance in Spain.* Berkeley: University of California Press, 1913.

Tiefenbrun, Susan W. "*La Belle Vieille* de François Maynard: Analyse sémiologique." *Cahiers Maynard* 8 (1978): 5–38.

———. "Mathurin Régnier's *Macette*: A Semiotic Study in Satire." In *Signs of the Hidden.* Amsterdam: Rodopi, 1980.

Weinberg, Bernard. "Du Bellay's 'Contre les Petrarquistes.'" *L'Esprit Créateur* 12 (1972): 159–77.

Wellek, René. *Concepts of Criticism.* New Haven: Yale University Press, 1963.

Wells, Henry. *Poetic Imagery: Illustrated from Elizabethan Literature.* New York: Columbia University Press, 1924.

Index